QUICK
PREP
SLOW
COOK

hamlyn

First published in Great Britain in 2024 by Hamlyn,
an imprint of Octopus Publishing Group Ltd
Carmelite House
50 Victoria Embankment
London EC4Y 0DZ
www.octopusbooks.co.uk

An Hachette UK Company
www.hachette.co.uk

Distributed in the US by
Hachette Book Group
1290 Avenue of the Americas
4th and 5th Floors
New York, NY 10104

Distributed in Canada by
Canadian Manda Group
664 Annette St. Toronto, Ontario, Canada M6S 2C8

ISBN 978 0 60063 845 2

Printed and bound in China.

10 9 8 7 6 5 4 3 2 1

Standard level spoon measurements are used in
all recipes.
1 tablespoon = one 15 ml spoon
1 teaspoon = one 5 ml spoon

Both imperial and metric measurements have been
given in all recipes. Use one set of measurements only
and not a mixture of both.

Eggs should be medium unless otherwise stated.

Milk should be full fat unless otherwise stated.

Fresh herbs should be used unless otherwise stated.
If unavailable use dried herbs as an alternative but
halve the quantities stated.

Pepper should be freshly ground black pepper unless
otherwise stated.

This book includes dishes made with nuts and nut
derivatives. It is advisable for those with known allergic
reactions to nuts and nut derivatives and those who
may be potentially vulnerable to these allergies, such as
pregnant and nursing mothers, the elderly, babies and
children, to avoid dishes made with nuts and nut oils.
It is also prudent to check the labels of pre-prepared
ingredients for the possible inclusion of nut derivatives.

Vegetarians should look for the 'V' symbol on a cheese
to ensure it is made with vegetarian rennet.

QUICK PREP SLOW COOK

100 slow cooker recipes

10 MINUTES' preparation

CHARLOTTE PIKE

hamlyn

Contents

Introduction

Slow cookers have to be one of the most useful, hard-working and inexpensive pieces of equipment you can have in the kitchen. They're very user-friendly, consume comparatively little energy, and offer a really practical way of preparing a wide range of food and drink to suit all manner of circumstances, from quick meals to have ready after a long day at work, to batch cooking and even entertaining.

This book aims to offer a broad range of really delicious recipes that, thanks to the slow cooker, will hopefully become regular additions to your repertoire. The aim is to keep the preparation time to an absolute minimum and to make the recipes as quick as possible to prepare with minimum equipment. Hopefully, they will gradually become even quicker to prepare as you familiarize yourself with the process. It is never easy to set a time limit on recipe prep, given that we all have different circumstances and skill levels.

There are varying levels of preparation throughout the book. The more involved recipes will take a little more time than the simplest, but they are really worth the effort. To help you along the way, it is always a good idea to read the recipe in full before starting and to find the ingredients you need. You may wish to preheat the slow cooker on high, to warm up as you work.

If chopping ingredients is a challenge for reasons of dexterity or time, then do use pre-prepared ingredients where possible. If neither applies, improving knife skills always helps to speed up your cooking. A sharp knife, a stable board and possibly watching a tutorial online will help. You will find some useful recommendations on pages 8–9.

Some recipes do recommend to briefly pan-fry some ingredients before starting. This helps improve the flavour of onions and spices. There is a detectable flavour difference in doing this, but if time is tight, the recipes will work without this step: just make sure they are cooked for long enough for the flavours to develop and the onions to become tender. There is one exception based on advice I have been given by Indian cooks: fresh curry leaves should always be fried in oil before using.

There are now a wide range of electric slow cookers available to buy, with varying features, and the amount of time they take to heat up differs. It's worth understanding which type you may wish to buy, or indeed may have already, and its functions to get the most out of it.

First, the simplest type of slow cooker. These tend to be the lower priced or older models. They have fewer functions, but they work extremely well. They have two temperature settings, low and high, plus a keep warm function. Setting them to high will mean they get really warm throughout the cooking time. The contents will get really hot and cook reasonably quickly, compared to the low setting, but they rarely get hot quickly. Therefore, you may wish to briefly pan-fry some of the core ingredients, such as onions, spices or meats in a frying pan first and then transfer the contents back into the slow cooker along with the additional ingredients. Alternatively, there are models available with hobproof cooking pots, which allow you to fry ingredients on the hob in the pot before transferring to the slow cooker, saving you valuable washing-up time.

A newer feature of many slow cookers is a searing or braising function, in addition to the high and low settings. This is very useful, and, if your budget allows, these models are really worth considering. They get hot very quickly and are so useful for flash-frying ingredients before setting them to cook on a lower heat. This function can also be used to give your dish a quick boost to speed up the cooking time, or if you need to heat it up fast.

There is also the multi-function cooker that features a slow cook setting. These are comparatively new and have a range of functions, from searing to even air-frying. They work fantastically well and are so useful for cooking efficiently. They are really useful for small kitchens or for cooking in compromised circumstances, such as the presence of builders.

Buy the size that suits your needs, but for this book, you need a minimum 2-litre (3½-pint) capacity. Larger models will work fine and indeed the recipes have been tested using much larger slow cookers. When buying kitchen kit of any sort, it is often useful to buy a larger capacity model than you need, so that you have the scope to cook on a bigger scale if needed.

7

Tips and Recommendations

Top ingredient recommendations

- Use **chopped frozen onions**, **squash** or **soffritto**.

- Substitute freshly grated root ginger with **ginger paste** or **frozen shredded fresh root ginger**.

- Swap fresh garlic with **garlic paste** or **frozen chopped garlic**. Around ½ teaspoon equates to 1 large clove.

- **Frozen herbs** work instead of fresh.

- When using herbs, **hard, fresh herbs** such as rosemary, thyme, sage, lime or curry leaves go in at the start. Add **soft, fresh herbs** such as parsley, coriander, dill, or tarragon at the end so they don't lose their colour or flavour.

- Add **root vegetables** at the start of the cooking time, as they take time to soften.

- Add **green vegetables** towards the end of the cooking time. They will keep their colour if the lid is not fully closed.

- Slow cooking is a great way of cooking cheaper and fattier **marbled cuts of meat**. These will often work better than leaner, more premium cuts.

- **Remove the skin from meat** before cooking.

- Fat-marbled meat works well in slow-cooked dishes, but **trim off any excess chunks of fat** from the meat before cooking.

- **To thicken sauces**, leave the lid ajar for any liquid to cook off, or use a Roux (see page 86).

- If you are using dairy products, **try to use full fat**. Reduced-fat products can be inclined to split.

Top equipment recommendations

- A **stick blender**, **blender** or **food processor**

- **Wooden spoons**, for non-scratch stirring

- A **ladle**, for serving

- A **silicone whisk**, for non-scratch whisking

- **Nonstick baking pa**per

- A **pudding basin**

Vegetarian

This dish comes from North Africa. It's full of flavour and the peppers are cooked until they are tender and sweet. Serve this at any time of the day, but it's particularly popular for brunch.

Shakshuka

1 teaspoon olive oil
1 teaspoon cumin seeds
2 shallots, thinly sliced
4 red, yellow or orange
  peppers, cored, deseeded
  and cut into strips
4 teaspoons caster sugar
2 ripe tomatoes, roughly
  chopped

4 eggs
2 tablespoons chopped
  parsley
2 tablespoons chopped
  fresh coriander
salt and pepper
fresh bread, to serve

1. Set the slow cooker to high. Add the oil, cumin seeds and shallots and warm through for a minute or two. Add the peppers, sugar and tomatoes and season with salt and pepper. Cover with the lid and cook on high for 1–2 hours until the peppers are tender. The mixture will look quite dry, which is ideal.

2. Fifteen minutes before you're ready to serve, add the eggs. Make four little wells in the peppers using the back of a spoon. Carefully crack the eggs, one at a time, into the wells. Season the eggs with a little sprinkle of salt.

3. Once the eggs have gone in, partially cover with the lid to allow any excess water to cook off. Cook on a very gentle heat for 10–15 minutes, or until the egg whites are set. Cook for longer if you'd like the yolks set. To serve, spoon out on to plates. Sprinkle with the parsley and coriander and serve with some fresh bread.

This easy recipe is so delicious and simple to prepare. It's ideal to make in a big batch if needed, and is adored by adults and children alike. If you'd prefer a dairy-free version, just leave out the mascarpone and grated cheese topping.

Tomato and Mascarpone Penne

1 tablespoon olive oil
6 garlic cloves, chopped
400 g (13 oz) can chopped tomatoes
500 ml (17 fl oz) vegetable stock (see page 113 for homemade)
400 g (13 oz) dried penne

1 teaspoon sea salt
plenty of pepper
1 teaspoon granulated sugar
1 heaped tablespoon mascarpone cheese (optional)
grated cheese, to serve

1. Set the slow cooker to high and add the oil and garlic. Warm through until fragrant.

2. Add the tomatoes and stir through, followed by the stock, penne and salt, pepper and sugar. Stir well, cover with the lid and cook on high for 30 minutes–1 hour until the pasta is cooked to your liking. If you're using mascarpone, stir it in just before serving. Taste, adjust the seasoning and serve, topped with some grated cheese.

TIP

Pasta brands do vary somewhat in cooking time. So it's best to check after 30 minutes, then check at 10-minute intervals.

Make this for a very quick lunch or dinner. It's packed full of flavour and so straightforward to put together. A warming, spicy hug in a bowl.

Harissa and Tomato Chickpea Stew
with Coriander Yogurt

2 tablespoons olive oil
4 garlic cloves, chopped
250 g (8 oz) tomatoes, chopped
2 x 400 g (13 oz) cans chickpeas
2 heaped tablespoons rose harissa
Zest of 1 unwaxed lemon, finely grated
salt

FOR THE CORIANDER YOGURT
25 g (1 oz) fresh coriander, chopped
pinch of salt
175 g (6 oz) thick yogurt, such as Greek yogurt

1. Place the oil, garlic, tomatoes, chickpeas, including their liquid, and the harissa into the slow cooker. Set to low, cover with the lid and cook for at least 3 hours until the sauce looks rich and glossy and has reduced a little.

2. Next, make the coriander yogurt by stirring the chopped coriander and salt into the yogurt. Store in the refrigerator until needed.

3. Taste the stew, and add a little salt if needed before serving.

4. Stir and serve the stew in bowls with some coriander yogurt and lemon zest spooned on top.

This is such a straightforward stew, which takes the vibrant flavours of tomatoes, chillies and garlic from an Arrabbiata pasta sauce and uses beans instead of pasta.

Butter Bean Arrabbiata Stew

2 tablespoons olive oil
4 garlic cloves, chopped
1 red chilli, deseeded
  and chopped
2 x 400 g (13 oz) cans butter
  beans, drained and rinsed
2 x 400 g (13 oz) cans
  chopped tomatoes

½ teaspoon sugar
1 teaspoon salt

TO SERVE
grated vegetarian Italian
  hard cheese, to taste
10 g (¼ oz) flat leaf
  parsley, chopped

1. Set the slow cooker to high. Add the oil, garlic and chilli and warm them through until they start to smell fragrant.

2. Then add the remaining ingredients, stir, cover with the lid and cook on low for at least 2 hours until the sauce is simmering and slightly thickened and the beans are fully heated through. Taste and adjust the seasoning if you need to. You might wish to add a little more salt or sugar.

3. Serve in bowls, topped with grated cheese and the parsley. Any leftovers will keep very well in the refrigerator for up to 5 days and will reheat quickly and successfully.

TIP

Butter beans work particularly well here, with their firmer texture, but you can use any white beans as an alternative.

This is a delicious, full-flavoured macaroni cheese. For even more flavour, substitute 50 g (2 oz) of the cheese with vegetarian Italian hard cheese. If you'd like a milder cheese flavour, perhaps for children, simply use a milder cheese and perhaps less pepper and mustard.

Macaroni Cheese

50 g (2 oz) butter
50 g (2 oz) plain flour
900 ml–1 litre (1½ –1¾ pints) milk
1 heaped teaspoon Dijon mustard
300 g (10 oz) mature Cheddar cheese, grated

½ teaspoon salt
plenty of pepper
400 g (13 oz) dried macaroni or pasta shapes

1. Set the slow cooker to high. Add the butter and allow it to melt. Then add the flour and stir it in to form a thick roux. Stir for a minute or two to cook the flour.

2. Next, add around 75 ml (3 fl oz) of the milk and stir in to form a smooth paste. Add the mustard and stir in, followed by the cheese, salt and pepper. Stir again.

3. Add the remaining milk and the pasta and stir again. Cover with the lid, set to cook on low for at least 2 hours until the pasta is cooked through and the sauce is smooth and richly flavoured from the cheese and mustard.

4. Serve straight from the slow cooker. Any leftovers will keep very well in the refrigerator for 3–5 days and will reheat quickly and successfully.

This lovely recipe combines spices, sweet fruit and contrasting citrus notes, producing a wonderfully warming dish redolent of Moroccan flavours. Prunes would make a nice alternative to dates.

VEGETARIAN

Chickpea, Date and Coriander Stew

1 large brown onion,
  finely chopped
6 garlic cloves, roughly
  chopped
1 tablespoon olive oil
1 teaspoon salt
generous grind of pepper
1 tablespoon ground cumin
1 tablespoon ground
  coriander
1 tablespoon ground ginger
1 cinnamon stick
2 x 400 g (13 oz) cans
  chickpeas, drained
  and rinsed

2 x 400 g (13 oz) cans
  chopped tomatoes
100 g (3½ oz) dates,
  pits removed and
  roughly chopped
1 unwaxed lemon, zest
  removed, either using a
  fine grater or thin strips
  using a potato peeler
25 g (1 oz) fresh coriander,
  roughly chopped

TO SERVE
thick yogurt
couscous (optional)

1. Quickly fry the onion and garlic in the olive oil in the slow cooker. If your slow cooker has the sear function, use this now. Add the salt, pepper and spices and fry for a couple of minutes to start to soften the onion and to cook the spices. If your slow cooker is slow to heat up, do this in a frying pan and transfer to the slow cooker after a couple of minutes.

2. Add the chickpeas, tomatoes, dates and lemon zest, stir well, cover and cook on high for 2 hours, ensuring the lid is firmly in place so that the steam is retained within the slow cooker. Stir a couple of times throughout cooking if you can.

3. Stir and taste the stew to check the seasoning. It will happily cook for longer on low and will keep warm for some time if needed. Add the coriander just before serving. Some yogurt makes a nice topping and couscous is a lovely optional accompaniment.

This Italian-inspired ragù makes a great sauce to serve with pasta, for a quick, healthy and tasty meal. Top with some freshly grated vegetarian Italian hard cheese.

Lentil Ragù

2 tablespoons olive oil, plus extra to serve
1 onion, sliced
6 garlic cloves, chopped
4 celery sticks, chopped
2 carrots, peeled and chopped
2 bay leaves
2 tablespoons tomato purée
400 g (13 oz) dried green lentils
300 ml (½ pint) passata (sieved tomatoes)
180 ml (6 fl oz) vegetable stock (see page 113 for homemade)
salt and pepper
cooked pasta, to serve (allow 60 g/2¼ oz dried pasta per adult)

1. If you have a sear or braise function on the slow cooker, switch it on and add the oil, followed by the onion, garlic, celery and carrots. Stir-fry for a couple of minutes to get the dish cooking.

2. If your slow cooker does not have this function, this can be done in a large frying pan, on a high heat. Once the ingredients have been cooked for a few minutes, transfer them to the slow cooker bowl.

3. Now, add all the remaining ingredients, seasoning with plenty of salt and pepper. Stir well. Cover with cold water, stir again and put the lid on. Cook on low for 2–4 hours until the lentils are very tender. Stir into cooked pasta before serving.

serves
4

This stew delivers a wonderfully fresh yet rich flavour – perfect for a cold day. It's a great complete meal in one and can be served with some fresh bread to mop up the juices. Adding the Parmesan rind is optional for non-vegetarians: it adds a wonderful richness, if you have one to use.

Squash, Cannellini Bean and Tomato Stew *with Pesto*

3 tablespoons olive oil
4 garlic cloves, chopped
1 medium squash, peeled, deseeded and cut into 1–2 cm (½–¾ inch) cubes
400 g (13 oz) can chopped tomatoes
400 g (13 oz) can cannellini beans, drained and rinsed

750 ml (1¼ pints) vegetable stock (see page 113 for homemade)
1 Parmesan cheese rind (optional)
salt and pepper
4 tablespoons vegetarian basil pesto
buttered toast, to serve

1. If you have a sear or braise function on the slow cooker, switch it on and add the oil, garlic and squash.

2. If your slow cooker does not have this function, simply turn it on to high at the earliest opportunity, add the oil, garlic and squash and allow a few minutes for the garlic to start to warm and become fragrant.

3. Next, add the tomatoes, beans and stock and season well. Add the Parmesan rind, if using it. Stir well, cover and cook on low for at least 4 hours until the sauce tastes rich and flavourful and the squash is completely tender.

4. Serve spooned into bowls, with a generous spoonful of pesto swirled through each one, and some buttered toast on the side.

serves
4

This is a wonderful rich and warming bean chilli. It's a really good recipe to leave slowly bubbling during the day. It can be served with rice, a baked potato or perhaps even some garlic bread. Fresh coriander and possibly a spoonful of soured cream make nice toppings, too.

Chilli sin Carne

1 tablespoon olive oil
1 white onion, finely
  chopped
4 garlic cloves, chopped
1 red chilli, deseeded
  and chopped
1 teaspoon ground cumin
1 teaspoon ground
  coriander
1 teaspoon ground
  cinnamon

3 x 400 g (13 oz) cans
  beans, such as red kidney
  beans, black beans
  or black-eyed beans,
  drained and rinsed
2 x 400 g (13 oz) cans
  chopped tomatoes
2 tablespoons tomato purée
1 teaspoon caster sugar
salt and pepper
rice, to serve

1. If you have a sear or braise function on the slow cooker, switch it on and add the oil, onion, garlic and chilli, followed by the spices, and fry for a couple of minutes to cook the spices and soften the onion.

2. If your slow cooker does not have this function, it is nice to do this in a large frying pan on a high heat. Once the ingredients start to smell fragrant, transfer the ingredients to the slow cooker.

3. Add the remaining ingredients, stir well, cover with the lid and leave to cook on low for at least 4 hours. Six or even 8 hours should be fine here. Taste and adjust the seasoning if you need to. Serve straight from the slow cooker with some rice. Any leftovers will keep well in the refrigerator, covered, for up to 5 days.

27

This stew is so warming and full of vibrant flavours and it feels as though it's doing you good. It's great served with some fresh bread and possibly a spoonful of thick yogurt on top.

Red Lentil, Turmeric, Lemon and Spinach Stew

1 large, brown onion, chopped
1 tablespoon olive oil
1 tablespoon fresh turmeric, peeled and grated or 1 heaped teaspoon dried
1 tablespoon peeled and grated fresh root ginger
1 tablespoon cumin seeds
350 g (11½ oz) dried red lentils
1.25 litres (2 pints) vegetable stock (see page 113 for homemade)
125 g (4 oz) fresh spinach leaves
freshly squeezed juice of ½ lemon
salt and pepper
bread and butter, to serve (optional)

1. If your slow cooker has the sear or braise function, use this now. Start by quickly frying the onion in the olive oil in the slow cooker or alternatively in a frying pan. Add the turmeric, ginger and cumin seeds and fry for a couple of minutes to start to soften the onion and to cook the spices.

2. If you need to transfer the mixture from a pan to the slow cooker, do this now, then add the lentils. Season generously with salt and pepper. Add the stock. Stir, cover with the lid and cook on low for at least 2 hours.

3. Just before you want to eat, add the spinach leaves and stir them in as they soften in the heat of the stew. Add the lemon juice and taste. Adjust the seasoning if needed and serve straight away, spooned into bowls, with some bread and butter on the side, if liked.

serves
4

If you like fresh, aromatic flavours, then this is the recipe for you. Add the noodles just before serving.

VEGETARIAN

Aromatic Squash Noodle Soup

1 tablespoon sunflower or rapeseed oil
1 shallot, thinly sliced
2 garlic cloves, chopped
4 tablespoons peeled and grated fresh root ginger
1 lemon grass stick, split in half
400 g (13 oz) squash, such as butternut, peeled, deseeded and cut into 1 cm (½ inch) cubes
5 fresh lime leaves (dried will work, too)
400 ml (14 fl oz) can full-fat coconut milk

400 ml (14 fl oz) vegetable stock, plus a little extra, if needed (see page 113 for homemade)
100 g (3½ oz) green beans, halved (optional)
90 g (3¼ oz) dried rice stick noodles, cooked according to pack instructions and drained
freshly squeezed lime juice, to taste
10 g (¼ oz) fresh coriander, chopped, to serve

1. If you have a sear or braise function on the slow cooker, switch it on and add the oil. Add the shallot, garlic and ginger and fry for just a minute until they smell fragrant.

2. If your slow cooker does not have this function, do this in a large frying pan, on a high heat. Cook for a few minutes, then transfer to the slow cooker bowl.

3. Add the lemon grass, squash, lime leaves, coconut milk and stock. Cover and cook on low for 1 hour, then check the squash is tender. It may need a little more time.

4. If you wish to add green beans, add them to the slow cooker around 15 minutes before you wish to serve.

5. Stir in the noodles just before serving. Add a dash of lime juice to taste, then remove the lemon grass pieces. Serve topped with the chopped coriander.

A hearty, wholesome soup, packed full of lovely pasta and beans and topped with pesto for an extra layer of flavour. This is great to make in a batch and reheat on demand, perhaps for a quick lunch.

Pasta e fagioli

1 tablespoon olive oil
1 large onion, thinly sliced
4 garlic cloves, chopped
1 leek, trimmed, cleaned
  and thinly sliced
1 carrot, peeled and
  finely diced
2 x 400 g (13 oz) cans
  borlotti beans, drained
  and rinsed
2 tablespoons chopped
  rosemary

100 g (3½ oz) dried pasta
  shapes, such as ditaloni
1.5 litres (2½ pints)
  vegetable stock
1 Parmesan cheese
  rind (optional)
75 g (3 oz) kale, chopped
  (optional)
salt and pepper
vegetarian basil pesto,
  to serve

1. If your slow cooker has a sear or braise function, switch it on and add the oil. Add the onion, garlic and leek and gently fry for a couple of minutes to start to cook them.

2. If your slow cooker does not have this function, it is nice to do this in a large frying pan, on a high heat. Cook the ingredients for a few minutes, then transfer to the slow cooker bowl.

3. Add the carrot, beans, rosemary, pasta, stock and the Parmesan rind, if using, and season with salt and pepper. Cover with the lid and cook on high for 1–2 hours.

4. The pasta is cooked after 1 hour, and will hold for another hour if needed. If you want to prepare this in advance, the base of the soup will happily cook for longer, and the pasta can be added around 1 hour before servng.

5. If you are using kale, stir it in just before serving. Remove the Parmesan rind if you have used it, then serve the soup ladled into bowls and topped with pesto.

Vegan *Ideas*

Braised Chickpeas with Tomatoes and Almonds

Set the slow cooker to high. Add 6 tablespoons **olive oil,** 2 x 400 g (13 oz) **cans chickpeas,** drained and rinsed, 2 **bay leaves,** 1 chopped **garlic clove,** 1 finely chopped **white onion,** 500 g (1 lb) **fresh, ripe tomatoes,** peeled and roughly chopped, **salt and pepper** and 100 ml (3½ fl oz) **vegetable stock.** Stir well, cover with the lid and cook on high for at least 2 hours. Serve topped with 50 g (2 oz) chopped **toasted almonds.**

Italian-style Green Lentils with Olive Oil and Herbs

Warm 2 tablespoons **olive oil** in the slow cooker, set to high. Add 1 sliced **onion,** 6 chopped **garlic cloves,** 4 chopped **celery sticks** and 2 peeled and chopped **carrots** and fry for a couple of minutes. Add 2 **bay leaves,** 1 tablespoon each of **thyme leaves** and **chopped rosemary,** 1 teaspoon **red wine vinegar, salt and pepper** and 400 g (13 oz) **dried green lentils** and just cover with water. Stir, cover and cook on low for 3–4 hours until the lentils are very tender. Serve warm, drizzled with olive oil and topped with 20 g (¾ oz) chopped **flat leaf parsley.**

Sweet Vegetable and Chickpea Stew

Set the slow cooker to high and add 1 teaspoon **sunflower oil,** 3 chopped **garlic cloves,** 1 tablespoon peeled and grated **fresh root ginger,** 1 teaspoon **cumin seeds** and 2 teaspoons **ground cinnamon.** Fry briefly to cook the spices. Add 2 teaspoons **tomato purée,** 400 g (13 oz) **can chopped tomatoes,** 400 g (13 oz) **can chickpeas,** drained and rinsed, 4 **red peppers,** cored, deseeded and chopped, 35 g (1¼ oz) **sultanas,** 75 ml (3 fl oz) **vegetable stock,** 2 teaspoons **maple syrup,** 2 tablespoons **lemon juice** and season with **salt and pepper.** Stir well, cover and cook on high for at least 4 hours until it tastes rich, fragrant and slightly sweet. Serve with couscous.

Butter Bean and Tomato Stew with Fresh Herbs

Set the slow cooker to high. Add 5 tablespoons **olive oil,** 6 chopped **garlic cloves,** 2 x 400 g (13 oz) **cans butter beans,** drained, 400 g (13 oz) **can chopped tomatoes,** 1 heaped teaspoon toasted **cumin seeds,** 1 teaspoon **maple or agave syrup** and season well with **salt and pepper.** Stir, cover and cook on low for at least 2 hours until the sauce tastes rich. Serve topped with the zest of 1 **unwaxed lemon** and 2 tablespoons each of **chopped flat leaf parsley** and **mint.**

Brazilian Black Bean Stew

Set the slow cooker to high. Add 2 tablespoons **olive oil**, 1 chopped **onion**, 4 chopped **garlic cloves**, 1 teaspoon each of **ground cumin, coriander** and **oregano**, 3 **bay leaves**, 1 tablespoon **tomato purée**, 400 g (13 oz) **can chopped tomatoes**, 2 x 400 g (13 oz) **cans black beans**, drained, 200 ml (7 fl oz) **canned coconut milk** and the zest of 1 **orange**. Stir, season with **salt and pepper** and cover with the lid. Cook on low for at least 4 hours. Taste, adjust the seasoning if needed and serve with rice.

Chickpea, Lemon and Coconut Stew

Put 1 tablespoon **olive oil** and 4 chopped **garlic cloves** into the slow cooker and set to high. Add 2 x 400 g (13 oz) **cans chickpeas**, drained and rinsed, and 1 tablespoon **ground turmeric** and stir through. Season with plenty of **salt and pepper**. Add 400 ml (14 fl oz) can **full-fat coconut milk** and the zest of 1 **unwaxed lemon** with 1 teaspoon **lemon juice**. Stir, put the lid on and cook on low for at least 1 hour until the sauce tastes flavoursome. Stir in 75 g (3 oz) chopped **kale** just before serving, so that it wilts. Serve topped with **fresh coriander**.

Homemade 'Baked' Beans

Put 1 tablespoon **olive oil** into the slow cooker and set to high. Add 1 finely chopped **shallot**, ¼ teaspoon each of **garam masala** and **paprika**. Stir and warm through. Next, add 2 x 400 g (13 oz) **cans butter beans**, drained and rinsed, 400 g (13 oz) **passata** (sieved tomatoes), 1 tablespoon **balsamic vinegar** and 2 tablespoons **maple syrup**. Season generously with **salt and pepper**. Stir, cover and cook on low for at least 4 hours until the beans are very tender and the sauce tastes savoury, sweet and rich all at once.

Mushroom and Chestnut Bourguignon

Put 750 g (1½ lb) sliced **mushrooms** into the slow cooker and set to high. Add 4 chopped **garlic cloves**, 2 peeled and sliced **carrots**, 8 small peeled **shallots**, ½ teaspoon **coriander seeds**, 1 tablespoon **black peppercorns**, 250 g (8 oz) cooked peeled **chestnuts**, 3 **bay leaves**, 3 **sprigs of thyme**, 3 **sprigs of rosemary**, 1 tablespoons **tomato purée**, 2 tablespoons **plain flour**, **salt and pepper**, ½ teaspoon **sugar**, 1 teaspoon **balsamic vinegar**, 250 ml (8 fl oz) **red wine** and 250 ml (8 fl oz) **vegetable stock**. Stir well. Cover, set to high and cook for at least 4 hours until the ingredients are tender and the sauce tastes rich. Serve with mashed potatoes.

Chicken

The flavour of coconut and turmeric is so delicious in this rich, creamy stew. This is a very popular recipe, and it's an especially good recipe to multiply to serve a crowd.

Spiced Coconut Chicken

1 tablespoon sunflower oil or ghee
1 large brown onion, thinly sliced
4 garlic cloves, chopped
40 g (1½ oz) fresh root ginger, peeled and grated
1 green chilli, deseeded and chopped
500 g (1lb) chicken thighs, skin and bones removed, trimmed and cut in half
1 teaspoon salt

1 teaspoon caster sugar
1 teaspoon ground turmeric
1 teaspoon ground cumin
1 teaspoon ground ginger
1 teaspoon ground cinnamon
250 ml (8 fl oz) boiling water
100 g (3½ oz) block creamed coconut
50 g (2 oz) desiccated coconut
basmati rice, to serve

1. If you have a sear or braise function on the slow cooker, switch it on and add the oil, onion, garlic, ginger and chilli, followed by the chicken, salt, sugar and spices, and then fry for a couple of minutes to start to get the dish cooking.

2. If your slow cooker does not have this function, it is worth taking the trouble to do this in a large frying pan, on a high heat. Once the ingredients start to smell fragrant, transfer them to the slow cooker.

3. Next, add the water and both types of coconut. Stir well and put the lid on the slow cooker. Cook on low for at least 3 hours until the chicken is very tender. The desiccated coconut will swell a little and the sauce will thicken as it cooks. Add a dash of water if necessary to loosen the sauce. Taste and adjust the seasoning before serving. You may want to add a little more salt or even sugar. Serve with rice.

serves
4

Inspired by the flavours of Spanish braised chicken dishes, which use plenty of olive oil, garlic, white wine and bay leaves, this light stew has a delicate yet complex flavour.

Chicken Stew
with White Wine, Garlic and Bay

2 tablespoons olive oil
500 g (1 lb) boneless, skinless chicken thighs
6 garlic cloves, chopped
4 bay leaves
100 ml (3½ fl oz) dry white wine
50 ml (2 fl oz) chicken stock (see page 113 for homemade)

25 g (1 oz) Roux (see page 86, optional)
1 tablespoon chopped flat leaf parsley

TO SERVE
rice, or boiled or mashed potatoes
green beans

1. If you have a sear or braise function on the slow cooker, switch it on and add the oil, chicken and garlic, then fry for a couple of minutes to start to get the dish cooking.

2. If your slow cooker does not have this function, it is worth taking the trouble to do this in a large frying pan, on a medium-high heat. Once the ingredients start to smell fragrant, transfer them to the slow cooker.

3. Add the bay leaves, wine and stock, cover with the lid and cook on low for at least 4 hours. If you would like a thicker sauce, add the roux, stir it in and allow at least 15 minutes for it to cook through. Serve the stew topped with the parsley, with rice or potatoes and green beans.

serves
4

Sopa de lima, as it's called in Mexico, is a wonderfully zingy yet light chicken soup. It works really well if you cook the chicken thighs with the bone in, then remove the bones just before serving.

Yucatán Citrus Chicken Broth
with Tortillas and Avocado

4 bone-in, skinless chicken
 thighs
6 garlic cloves, chopped
1 green chilli, deseeded
 and chopped
4 large tomatoes, chopped
1 teaspoon allspice berries
1 tablespoon thyme leaves
zest and juice of 3 limes
zest and juice of 1 pink
 grapefruit
300 ml (½ pint) chicken
 stock (see page 113
 for homemade)

½–1 teaspoon salt, to taste
1–2 teaspoons pepper,
 to taste

TO SERVE
1 ripe avocado, diced
15 g (½oz) fresh coriander,
 chopped
2 handfuls of salted corn
 tortilla chips or totopos

1. Place all the soup ingredients into the slow cooker, stir, put the lid on and cook on low for at least 4 hours until the chicken is falling apart.

2. Remove the bones from the chicken, and fish out the allspice berries, if you would prefer not to serve them whole (they are fine to eat).

3. Taste the broth and add more salt or pepper if you feel it needs it.

4. Serve ladled into bowls, topped generously with the avocado, fresh coriander and tortillas or totopos.

43

serves
4

The combination of sweet and savoury works so well in this popular Mediterranean chicken dish. Prunes can be used as an alternative to dates.

Chicken Marbella

500 g (1 lb) boneless, skinless chicken thighs, quartered
6 garlic cloves, chopped
1 tablespoon finely chopped oregano leaves
3 tablespoons red wine vinegar
3 tablespoons olive oil
75 g (3 oz) pitted green olives
50 g (2 oz) capers in brine, drained
75 g (3 oz) Medjool dates, pitted and roughly chopped

2 bay leaves
125 ml (4 fl oz) dry white wine
salt and pepper

TO SERVE
1 tablespoon date syrup (optional)
10 g (¼ oz) flat leaf parsley, chopped
basmati rice or orzo
green vegetables, such as green beans or broccoli

1. Set the slow cooker to low. Add all the ingredients to the slow cooker, stir well, put the lid on and cook for 2–4 hours until the chicken is very tender. There won't be lots of liquid left with this dish, but give it a good stir, so all the flavourings are evenly distributed.

2. Serve hot, drizzled with the date syrup, if using, and sprinkled with fresh parsley, plus rice and fresh vegetables on the side.

serves
4

This is a wonderfully easy complete meal in the slow cooker. The sauce is light but creamy and full of fragrance from the fresh tarragon. You don't have to add potatoes, but they cook very well in the sauce, taking on plenty of flavour.

Tarragon Chicken
with Cream, Shallots and Potatoes

25 g (1 oz) butter
1 large or 2 small shallots, finely sliced
500 g (1 lb) boneless, skinless chicken thighs, trimmed
75 ml (3 fl oz) dry white wine
75 ml (3 fl oz) double cream

500 g (1 lb) baby potatoes
25 g (1 oz) Roux (see page 86, optional)
2 tablespoons chopped tarragon
salt and pepper
green vegetables, to serve (optional)

1. Start by setting the slow cooker to high and adding the butter and shallots. Season well.

2. Allow the butter to melt and the shallots to start to soften and smell enticing. This should take a couple of minutes.

3. Next, add the chicken, wine and cream, cover with the lid and cook on low for at least 3 hours until the chicken is very tender. Add the potatoes and cook for another 1–1½ hours until they are tender.

4. If you prefer a thicker sauce, add the roux, stir it in and allow at least 15 minutes for it to cook through.

5. Taste and adjust the seasoning, if necessary, perhaps with a little more salt or pepper. Add the chopped tarragon and stir through. Serve hot, perhaps with a green vegetable on the side.

46

serves
4

This is a simple and quite traditional casserole that is full of flavour and wonderfully warming on a cold day. To save even more time, you can add some peeled potatoes to the casserole towards the end. It's great served with mashed potatoes, too, and perhaps a green vegetable.

Warming Chicken Casserole
with Root Vegetables and Herbs

50 g (2 oz) butter
500 g (1 lb) chicken thighs, skin and bones removed and cut in half
2 large brown onions, quartered
2 celery sticks, cut into large chunks
2 carrots, peeled and cut into large chunks
1 small swede, peeled and cut into large chunks
2 tablespoons plain flour
4 sprigs of thyme, leaves picked

350 ml (12 fl oz) chicken stock (see page 113 for homemade)
400 g (13 oz) floury potatoes, peeled and cut into large chunks (optional)
salt and plenty of pepper
10 g (¼ oz) flat leaf parsley, chopped, to serve

1. Set the slow cooker to high. Add the butter and allow it to melt. Next, add the chicken, onions, celery, carrots and swede and season with salt and pepper. Stir well to ensure all the ingredients are coated in the melted butter. Add the flour and stir through the stew ingredients, followed by the thyme and stock.

2. Cover with the lid and cook the stew on low for at least 4 hours, but 6 or 8 hours will work well, too.

3. If you wish to add potatoes, do this 1 hour before serving by which time the chicken should be very tender and should have fallen apart. Taste the sauce and add a little more seasoning, if desired.

4. Serve topped with the chopped parsley and any accompanying green vegetables.

47

serves
4

This slow-cooked chicken dish comes from Puebla in Mexico. It's absolutely full of flavour with some smokiness from the chorizo and chilli, which pair so well with the chicken and tomato. It is best served with either rice or in a taco. Use either cured or fresh chorizo in this recipe.

Chicken Tinga Poblana

1 tablespoon sunflower or rapeseed oil

1 onion, thinly sliced

4 garlic cloves, chopped

1 red chilli, deseeded and chopped

500 g (1 lb) boneless, skinless chicken thighs, trimmed, if necessary

150 g (5 oz) cured or fresh chorizo, sliced

1 heaped tablespoon ground cumin

1 dried chipotle chilli (optional)

4 bay leaves

1 heaped teaspoon dried oregano

1 teaspoon light brown soft sugar

1 teaspoon salt

400 g (13 oz) can chopped tomatoes

TO SERVE
rice or tacos
lime wedges

1. If you have a sear or braise function on the slow cooker, switch it on and add the oil, onion, garlic and fresh red chilli, followed by the chicken, chorizo, spices and herbs, then fry for a couple of minutes to start to get the dish cooking.

2. If your slow cooker does not have this function, it is worth taking the trouble to do this in a large frying pan, on a high heat. Once the ingredients start to smell fragrant, transfer them to the slow cooker.

3. Next, add the sugar, salt and tomatoes. Stir well, put the lid on and cook on low for at least 4 hours until the chicken is falling apart and the sauce is rich. Taste and check the seasoning. Serve hot with your choice of accompaniments.

serves
4

This is a wonderfully fruity stew. Toasting the walnuts really makes a difference to the flavour. Toast them either in a frying pan or on a baking sheet in a preheated oven, 180°C (350°F), Gas Mark 4 for around 8 minutes until they are slightly crisped and lightly browned.

Chicken Stew
with Walnuts and Pomegranate

600 g (1¼ lb) boneless, skinless chicken thighs
2 large brown onions, thinly sliced
75 ml (3 fl oz) olive oil
2 tablespoons ground cinnamon
1 tablespoon caster sugar
100 ml (3½ fl oz) pomegranate molasses
250 ml (8 fl oz) chicken stock (see page 113 for homemade)

150 g (5 oz) walnut pieces
salt and pepper

TO SERVE
basmati rice
seeds of ½ pomegranate (optional)
20 g (¾ oz) flat leaf parsley, chopped (optional)

1. If you have a sear or braise function on the slow cooker, switch it on. Start by quickly frying the chicken and onions in the olive oil in the slow cooker. Alternatively, this can be done in a frying pan. Fry for around 5 minutes until the onions have started to soften slightly and the chicken is lightly sealed.

2. If you need to transfer the mix back from a pan to the slow cooker, do this now and then add the cinnamon. Season well with salt and pepper and add the sugar, pomegranate molasses and chicken stock.

3. Stir well, place the lid on the slow cooker and cook on high for at least 2 hours until the chicken and onions are tender. Toast the walnuts in a dry frying pan on a medium-high heat until they smell nutty. This should take around 3 minutes. Add to the slow cooker once toasted and stir in.

4. Serve the stew with rice, topped with the pomegranate seeds and parsley, if you like.

TIP

Fresh coriander or dill would make nice alternatives to the parsley for topping.

serves
4

A simple, healthy and richly-flavoured stew, which is light to eat and vibrant in flavour.

Turmeric Chicken Stew
with Ginger and Spinach

1 teaspoon sunflower, rapeseed or coconut oil
500 g (1 lb) boneless, skinless chicken thighs, trimmed, if necessary
4 garlic cloves, chopped
20 g (¾ oz) fresh root ginger, peeled and grated
1 tablespoon turmeric, either ground, or fresh root, peeled and grated

generous pinch of sea salt
plenty of pepper
200 ml (7 fl oz) water
75 g (3 oz) fresh spinach leaves
10 g (¼ oz) fresh coriander, chopped (optional)
basmati rice, to serve

1. If you have a sear or braise function on the slow cooker, switch it on and add the oil, chicken, garlic, ginger and turmeric and fry for a couple of minutes to start to get the dish cooking.

2. If your slow cooker does not have this function, it is worth taking the trouble to do this in a large frying pan, on a high heat. Once the ingredients start to smell fragrant, transfer them to the slow cooker.

3. Add the salt, pepper and measured water, stir and cover with the lid. Cook on low for 4 hours until the chicken is very tender. Add the spinach leaves just before serving. Stir into the hot chicken, and they will quickly wilt. Serve, with rice, topped with the fresh coriander, if desired.

serves
4

This stew couldn't be easier to put together and produces a light but full-flavoured stew. It is very nice served with mashed potatoes and vegetables.

Chicken Marsala Stew

2 tablespoons olive oil
500 g (1 lb) boneless, skinless chicken thighs, trimmed and cut into large chunks
2 shallots, peeled and halved
4 garlic cloves, chopped
1 tablespoon chopped rosemary (fresh or dried)
250 g (8 oz) chestnut mushrooms, sliced

125 ml (4 fl oz) Marsala
100 ml (3½ fl oz) beef stock (see page 113 for homemade)
1 teaspoon tomato purée
salt and pepper
15 g (½ oz) flat leaf parsley, chopped, to garnish
mashed potatoes and/ or vegetables, to serve (optional)

1. If you have a sear or braise function on the slow cooker, switch it on and add the oil. Add the chicken, shallots, garlic, rosemary and mushrooms nd briefly fry for around 3 minutes.

2. If your slow cooker does not have this function, it is nice to do this in a large frying pan, on a high heat. Although this stew does work if time is short and you skip this step.

3. If you need to transfer the contents of the pan to the slow cooker, do this now. Then add all the remaining ingredients, except the parsley, cover and cook on low for at least 4 hours until the chicken is falling apart and the sauce tastes rich and well-balanced. Have a taste and add a little more salt and pepper if you feel it needs it.

4. Stir in the parsley just before serving, and spoon on to plates or into bowls. Serve with mashed potatoes and/ or vegetables, if desired. Any leftovers will keep in the refrigerator for 5 days and will reheat very nicely.

serves
4

If you like savoury, spicy flavours, then this wonderful dish will hopefully appeal. It's really good served with couscous or bulgur wheat, into which you could stir some chopped mint, parsley or fresh coriander.

Chicken
with Preserved Lemon, Harissa and Olives

1 tablespoon olive oil
4 garlic cloves, chopped
600 g (1¼ lb) boneless,
  skinless chicken thighs,
  trimmed
1 tablespoon rose harissa
½ teaspoon salt

1 preserved lemon,
  thinly sliced
50 g (2 oz) green olives,
  pitted
100 ml (3½ fl oz) water
couscous or bulgur wheat,
  to serve (optional)

1. Simply place all the ingredients in the slow cooker and set to high. Cover with the lid and cook for at least 2 hours until the chicken is falling apart and the sauce tastes rich.

2. Serve on its own or with couscous or bulgur wheat.

This is a really hearty, warming chicken casserole to enjoy on a cold day. It is packed full of comforting flavours and is so straightforward to make.

Chicken, Bacon and Mushroom Stew
with Cheddar and Mustard Dumplings

25 g (1 oz) butter
1 large onion, cut into
    wedges
500 g (1 lb) boneless,
    skinless chicken thighs
125 g (4 oz) smoked streaky
    bacon rashers, chopped
250 g (8 oz) small brown
    mushrooms, sliced
2 tablespoons plain flour
2 bay leaves
1 teaspoon dried thyme
400 ml (14 fl oz) chicken
    stock (see page 113
    for homemade)

salt and pepper
15 g (½ oz) parsley,
    chopped, to serve

FOR THE DUMPLINGS
175 g (6 oz) self-raising
    flour
pinch of salt
1 teaspoon English mustard
    powder or Dijon mustard
100 g (3½ oz) mature
    Cheddar cheese, grated
90 g (3¼ oz) suet
150 ml (¼ pint) cold water

1. Place all the ingredients for the stew into the slow cooker and set to high. Stir well, cover with the lid and cook for at least 4 hours until the chicken is very tender.

2. Around 1 hour before you want to eat, make the dumplings. Place the flour, salt, mustard, cheese and suet in a bowl and stir together. Add the measured water and bring together to form a stiff, slightly sticky dough. Divide into 8 pieces and roll into balls. Sit the dumpling balls evenly on top of the stew in the slow cooker, pushing them down so they are around three-quarters submerged in the liquid.

3. Replace the lid and cook on high for at least 45 minutes until the dumplings are fully cooked. They will be firm and a little shiny-looking on top, and some air bubbles will be visible. Sprinkle over the parsley and serve.

Soups *Ideas*

Carrot and Coriander Soup

Set the slow cooker to high and add 1 tablespoon **olive oil**, 1 chopped **onion** , 450 g (14½ oz) peeled and chopped **carrots** and 1 tablespoon **coriander seeds**. Next, fry these ingredients for a couple of minutes, season with **salt and pepper** and add 1.2 litres (2 pints) of **chicken or vegetable stock**. Stir, cover and cook on high for at least 1 hour until the carrots are tender. Blend and serve hot.

Minestrone

Warm 1 tablespoon **olive oil** in the slow cooker, set to high. Add 1 diced **onion**, 3 chopped **garlic cloves**, 1 finely sliced **leek**, 1 peeled and diced **carrot** and 2 thinly sliced **smoked bacon rashers** (optional). Fry for 2–3 minutes, then add 400 g (13 oz) **can chopped tomatoes**, 400 g (13 oz) **can cannellini beans**, drained and rinsed, 100 g (3½ oz) **small dried pasta shapes** and 1.2 litres (2 pints) **chicken or vegetable stock**. If you have a **Parmesan cheese rind**, add that in. Season with **salt and pepper**, cover and cook on high for 2–4 hours until the pasta is cooked and the liquid tastes flavoursome. Add 100 g (3½ oz) finely sliced **kale** just before serving, if desired. Serve topped with grated **Parmesan**.

Lamb Harira

Put 50 g (2 oz) **butter**, 1 sliced large **onion**, 4 chopped **garlic cloves**, 2 **bay leaves**, 1 teaspoon each of **ground cumin**, **turmeric**, **cinnamon** and **ginger**, 2 teaspoons **salt**, 2 tablespoons **rose harissa**, 300 g (10 oz) boneless, trimmed **lamb neck**, sliced, 400 g (13 oz) **can chickpeas**, 200 g (7 oz) **dried green lentils** and 400 g (13 oz) **can chopped tomatoes** into the slow cooker. Stir well. Add the juice of ½ **lemon**. Add enough water to cover by 3 cm (1¼ inches). Cover and cook on low for at least 4 hours until tender and rich. Serve generously topped with chopped **fresh coriander**.

Red Lentil Soup with Turmeric

Set the slow cooker to high and add 1 tablespoon **olive oil**, then 2 teaspoons ground or fresh, peeled and grated **turmeric**. Season with **salt and pepper** and fry for a couple of minutes. Next, add 225 g (7½ oz) **dried red lentils** and 1.2 litres (2 pints) **chicken or vegetable stock**. Cover and cook on low for around 2 hours until the lentils are tender. Add the juice of ½ **lemon** and blend the soup, if desired. Taste, adjust the seasoning if needed and serve.

Tomato, Chickpea and Kale Soup

Set the slow cooker to high and add 3 tablespoons **olive oil**, 1 chopped **onion**, 2 chopped **celery sticks**, 4 chopped **garlic cloves** and 1 **red chilli**, deseeded and chopped. Season with **salt and pepper** and fry for a couple of minutes. Now, add 400 g (13 oz) **can chickpeas**, drained and rinsed, 400 g (13 oz) **can chopped tomatoes** and 800 ml (1⅓ pints) **chicken or vegetable stock**. Stir, cover and cook on high for at least 2 hours until the chickpeas are tender. Blend lightly, add 100 g (3½ oz) finely chopped **kale leaves**, stirring them in until they wilt. Serve warm in bowls, topped with grated **Parmesan**.

Smoked Haddock Chowder

Add 25 g (1 oz) **butter** and 6 thinly sliced **spring onions** to the slow cooker, then set to high. Melt the butter and cook the spring onions for a couple of minutes to start to soften.

Add 500 g (1lb) **floury potatoes**, peeled and cut into 2 cm (¾ inch) chunks, 300 g (10 oz) **smoked haddock**, skin and bones removed, 200 g (7 oz) canned, drained **sweetcorn** and 500 ml (17 fl oz) **milk**. Season with **salt and pepper**, going lightly on the salt but heavily on the pepper, if you like. Stir well, put the lid on and simmer on low for at least 1½ hours until the potatoes are very tender and the haddock has broken up into flakes.

Season to taste. Add 1–2 tablespoons **cream**, if you wish. Stir in 20 g (¾ oz) chopped **flat leaf parsley or chives** and serve.

Bacon and Lentil Soup

Set the slow cooker to high and add 1 tablespoon **olive oil**, 1 diced **onion**, 2 chopped **garlic cloves**, 2 peeled and diced **carrots**, 2 diced **celery sticks**, 6 finely chopped **smoked bacon rashers**. Season with **salt and pepper** and fry for a couple of minutes. Add 400 g (13 oz) **can chopped tomatoes**, 600 ml (1 pint) **chicken or vegetable stock**, 1 **bay leaf** and 175 g (6 oz) **dried green lentils**. Stir, cover and cook on high for 1–2 hours until the lentils are tender. Season to taste and serve.

Thai-style Pumpkin Soup

Warm 1 tablespoon **sunflower oil** in the slow cooker, set to high. Add 900 g (1¾ lb) **pumpkin (or squash)**, peeled, deseeded and diced, 1 finely chopped **onion**, 1 tablespoon **Thai green curry paste**, ½ teaspoon **salt**, 1 teaspoon **palm or brown sugar**. Fry for 2–3 minutes, then add 500 ml (17 fl oz) **chicken or vegetable stock** and 400 ml (14 fl oz) can **full-fat coconut milk**. Stir, cover and cook on high for 1–2 hours until the squash is tender. Add the juice of ½ **lime** and blend. Taste, adding more sugar or salt if needed. Serve topped with **fresh coriander**.

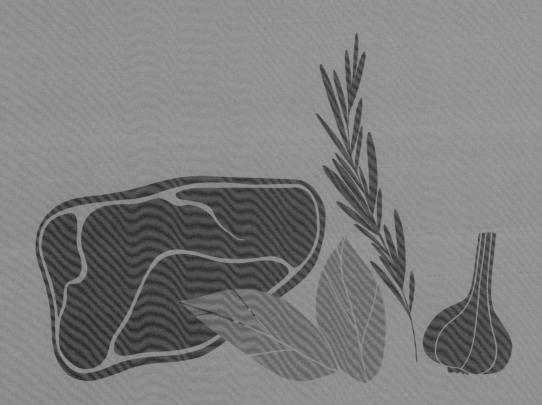

Meat

serves
4

This is a wonderful slow-cooked Mexican lamb dish, which makes a sensational filling for tacos. It is lovely served with the toppings suggested, or just some fresh coriander on its own. It is also very good as a slow-cooked meat with rice.

Vallarta Lamb Birria Tacos

50 g (2 oz) butter
500 g (1 lb) lamb shoulder, trimmed and cut into 2 cm (¾ inch) cubes
2 red onions, thinly sliced
4 garlic cloves, chopped
1 red chilli, deseeded and chopped
1 teaspoon dried oregano
1 teaspoon apple cider vinegar
2 bay leaves
1 teaspoon ground cumin
1 teaspoon ground allspice
½ teaspoon whole cloves
1 teaspoon salt

½ teaspoon black peppercorns
200 ml (7 fl oz) chicken, lamb or vegetable stock (see page 113 for homemade)

TO SERVE
at least 8 soft tacos or tortillas, warmed
½ red onion, thinly sliced
freshly squeezed juice of 1 lime
soured cream
10 g (¼ oz) fresh coriander, chopped

1. If you have a sear or braise function on the slow cooker, switch it on and add the butter, followed by the lamb, onions, garlic and chilli, then all the flavourings, including the salt and peppercorns. Fry for a couple of minutes to start to get the dish cooking.

2. If your slow cooker does not have this function, this can be done in a large frying pan, on a high heat. Once the ingredients have been cooked for a few minutes, transfer them to the slow cooker.

3. Add the stock to the slow cooker bowl, cover with the lid and cook on low for at least 4 hours until the meat falls apart and the sauce tastes rich and complex.

4. Serve hot, spooned into warm tacos with some red onion, lime juice, soured cream and fresh coriander.

A traditional-style beef casserole with a rich sauce, flavoured with stock, tomatoes and wine. Dumplings are particularly good added to this dish.

Beef Casserole

2 tablespoons olive oil
1 large onion, thinly sliced
600 g (1¼ lb) prepared beef, such as chuck or braising steak, cut into 2–3 cm (¾–1¼ inch) cubes
1 tablespoon plain flour
4 bay leaves
1 tablespoon Worcestershire sauce
1 tablespoon tomato purée
400 g (13 oz) carrots, peeled and cut on an angle into 1 cm (½ inch)-thick slices

175 ml (6 fl oz) beef stock (see page 113 for homemade)
250 ml (8 fl oz) red wine
Dumplings (see page 87, optional)
salt and pepper
flat leaf parsley, chopped, to garnish (optional)
green vegetables and/or mashed potatoes, to serve (optional)

TIP

Freshly cooked green vegetables and/or some mashed potatoes make a great accompaniment to this rich beef stew.

1. If you have a sear or braise function on the slow cooker, switch it on, then add the oil, onion, beef and flour and fry for a couple of minutes.

2. If your slow cooker does not have this function, do this in a large frying pan, on a high heat. However, if you are in a hurry, this isn't absolutely essential. Once the onion starts to smell fragrant, transfer the ingredients to the slow cooker.

3. Season with salt and pepper, then add the bay leaves, Worcestershire sauce, tomato purée, carrots, stock and wine and stir well. Cover with the lid and cook on low for at least 4 hours until the sauce has become rich and a little thicker, and the beef and vegetables are very tender.

4. If you wish to add dumplings, do so now and cook for a further 30–45 minutes until they are fully cooked.

5. Rest for 10 minutes, then serve with parsley, if desired.

serves
4

Lamb pairs so well with the Mediterranean-inspired flavours in this stew. It's deep, rich, sweet and savoury, all at once.

Rosemary and Olive Lamb Stew

1 tablespoon olive oil
1 brown onion, very
    thinly sliced
6 garlic cloves, roughly
    chopped
500 g (1 lb) lamb leg or
    shoulder, trimmed well
    and diced
250 ml (8 fl oz) dry white
    wine
400 g (13 oz) can chopped
    tomatoes

1 teaspoon caster sugar
100 g (3½ oz) black olives,
    pitted
25 g (1 oz) rosemary, leaves
    picked and roughly
    chopped
salt and pepper
mashed potatoes and/or a
    green vegetable, to serve

1. If you have a sear or braise function on the slow cooker, switch it on and add the oil. Quickly soften the onion and garlic in the hot bowl until browned on all sides. This should take around 2 minutes. Add the lamb and sear for another 2–3 minutes. Season well with salt and pepper.

2. If your slow cooker does not have this function, it is nice to do this in a large frying pan, on a high heat. It is not essential, if time and facilities do not permit. Transfer the lamb mixture to the slow cooker once browned.

3. Add all the remaining ingredients, cover and cook the stew on high for at least 2 hours until the lamb is very tender. It should fall apart. Taste and adjust the seasoning if needed.

4. Serve with mashed potatoes and/or a green vegetable.

This is a fantastic Brazilian-inspired pork and bean stew. Serve it with rice, baked potatoes, or just some greens for a warming and richly-flavoured meal.

Feijoada

1 tablespoon sunflower or rapeseed oil
1 large white onion, finely chopped
2 garlic cloves, chopped
1 red chilli, deseeded and finely chopped
600 g (1¼ lb) pork shoulder, trimmed and cut into 3 cm (1¼ inch) cubes
300 g (10 oz) fresh or cured chorizo, cut into 1 cm (½ inch) slices
100 g (3½ oz) smoked back bacon, chopped

400 g (13 oz) can black beans, drained and rinsed
1 teaspoon thyme leaves
4 bay leaves
1 teaspoon red wine vinegar
200 ml (7 fl oz) chicken stock (see page 113 for homemade)
freshly squeezed juice of 1 orange
salt and pepper (optional)
15 g (½ oz) fresh coriander, chopped, to garnish

1. If you have a sear or braise function on the slow cooker, switch it on and add the oil, onion, garlic and red chilli, followed by the pork, chorizo and bacon, then fry for a couple of minutes to start to get the dish cooking.

2. If your slow cooker does not have this function, it is worth taking the trouble to do this in a large frying pan, on a high heat. Once the ingredients start to smell fragrant, transfer them to the slow cooker.

3. Add the beans, thyme, bay leaves, vinegar and stock, cover with a lid and cook on low for at least 4 hours until the pork is very tender and the sauce tastes well-balanced. The fat and paprika from the chorizo will have added a rich, red colour. Add the orange juice and stir in. Taste, add salt or pepper if it needs it, and serve, topped with fresh coriander.

This is a wonderful, simple meal that's full of flavour.

If you can get good Italian sausages, please do use them. There are some wonderful varieties with fennel in, but don't worry if not. Good-quality plain pork sausages will work very well indeed.

Italian Lentils
with Sausages and Chilli

6–8 pork sausages, depending on appetite
3 tablespoons olive oil
1 onion, finely chopped
1 carrot, peeled and finely chopped
2 celery sticks, finely chopped
3 garlic cloves, chopped
3 bay leaves
1 teaspoon fennel seeds
pinch of dried chilli flakes

250 g (8 oz) dried Italian lentils, such as Castelluccio (small brown lentils)
150 ml (¼ pint) red wine
150 ml (¼ pint) vegetable or chicken stock (see page 113 for homemade)
salt and pepper
20 g (¾ oz) flat leaf parsley, chopped, to garnish

1. If your slow cooker has the sear or braise function, use this now. Start by quickly frying the sausages in the olive oil in the slow cooker. Alternatively, you can do this in a frying pan. Keep them turning so that they don't stick, and try and get a rich, brown colour on all sides. You may be able to do this while you prepare the vegetables.

2. Next, add the onion, carrot and celery – or soffritto – to the cooker or pan, together with the garlic, bay leaves, fennel seeds and chilli flakes. Fry for a minute or two, seasoning well.

3. If you need to transfer the mixture from a pan to the slow cooker, do this now, then add the lentils, wine and stock. Stir, cover with the lid and cook on low for at least 2 hours until the lentils are tender and the sausages are cooked through.

4. Taste, add a little more salt or pepper if you fancy it and serve with the chopped parsley on top.

TIP

To save chopping time here, you could use 350 g (11½ oz) prepared soffritto as a substitute for the onion, carrot and celery.

This is an extremely useful recipe to make in the slow cooker. It makes a super pasta sauce but it can also be used to make a lasagne. It multiplies very well too, perhaps to feed a crowd or freeze in smaller portions. More stock can be substituted for the wine if preferred.

MEAT

Beef Ragù

2 tablespoons olive oil
1 large white onion, sliced
4 garlic cloves, chopped
500 g (1 lb) minced beef
1 carrot, peeled and
    finely chopped
4 tablespoons
    concentrated tomato
    purée

100 ml (3½ fl oz) beef
    stock (see page 113
    for homemade)
150 ml (¼ pint) red wine
400 g (13 oz) can chopped
    tomatoes
1 bay leaf
plenty of salt and pepper

1. If you have a sear or braise function on the slow cooker, switch it on and add the oil, onion, garlic and beef and fry for a couple of minutes.

2. If your slow cooker does not have this function, set it to high and fry these ingredients separately in a frying pan if you have time, then transfer them to the slow cooker.

3. Add all the remaining ingredients and stir together well, ensuring the dish is well seasoned. Cover with the lid and cook on high for at least 4 hours until it's rich and slightly thickened. This beef ragù will very happily cook for longer if you want to leave it cooking.

makes
1
large cooked ham

Gently simmering the gammon in cider, apple juice and spices makes an absolutely delectable ham. Once cooked, it can be sliced and eaten straight away, or chilled and sliced on demand. When shopping, look for a raw gammon joint, either smoked or unsmoked.

Ham in Cider

1–1.5 kg (2–3 lb) gammon joint
500 ml (17 fl oz) cider
1 litre (1¾ pints) good-quality apple juice

1 heaped teaspoon black peppercorns
2 bay leaves
1 heaped teaspoon whole cloves (optional)

1. Sit the gammon in the slow cooker and add the remaining ingredients. Cover with the lid and cook on low for 2–4 hours until fully cooked. The best way to check if it's cooked is to stick a skewer into the centre of the ham. Lift the skewer up. If the ham slides straight back down into the liquid, it is cooked. If you meet some resistance and the ham sticks to the skewer, it will need more cooking until it gets to that point.

2. If you wish to eat the ham hot, remove it from the liquid, carve and serve. If you would rather keep it for another day, allow it to cool in the liquid, before removing the ham and keeping it wrapped and chilled. It works best to slice the ham on demand, as it will dry out if it is sliced in advance. Keep it in the refrigerator for up to 5 days.

Beef cheeks are fairly easy to get hold of in the supermarkets and most butchers sell them. They are a fantastic cut of beef to cook very slowly, especially in a slow cooker, but any type of stewing or casserole beef will work well as an alternative.

Braised Beef Cheeks
with Soy, Spices and Ginger

1 kg (2 lb) beef cheeks (approx. 2 large cheeks)
10 garlic cloves, chopped
50 g (2 oz) fresh root ginger, peeled and sliced
2 star anise
2 tablespoons light soy sauce, plus extra (optional) to serve

600 ml (1 pint) beef stock (see page 113 for homemade)
2 tablespoons clear honey (optional)
rice and/or a green vegetable, to serve

1. Simply place all the ingredients in the slow cooker, cover with the lid and set to cook on low for 6 hours. Turn the beef a couple of times throughout the cooking period if you can, so that it cooks a little more evenly. It doesn't matter too much if you are unable to do this.

2. Once cooked, the meat should fall apart when touched. Season to taste with more soy and honey if needed. Serve with rice and/or a green vegetable of your choice. You may like a touch more soy sauce on the top when it's plated up.

MEAT

TIP

This warming and fragrant beef dish is great served with rice and a green vegetable, perhaps pak choi or broccoli.

serves
4–6

A delicious slow-cooked pork dish, great served with buttery mashed potatoes or white beans, cooked with olive oil and rosemary. If you're tight on time, add a can of cannellini beans or some peeled, chopped potatoes to the cooking liquid with the pork for the final hour.

Braised Shoulder of Pork
with White Wine, Bay and Black Pepper

1 tablespoon olive oil
1 kg (2 lb) piece of pork shoulder, skin and excess fat removed along with any string
6 garlic cloves, peeled
1 heaped teaspoon salt
1 tablespoon black peppercorns
2 celery sticks, cut into 3 cm (1¼ inch) chunks

4 bay leaves
300 ml (½ pint) white wine
200 ml (7 fl oz) chicken, pork or vegetable stock (see page 113 for homemade)
mashed potatoes, white beans (see intro) or leafy greens, to serve

1. If you have a sear or braise function on the slow cooker, switch it on and add the oil. Fry the pork in the hot bowl until browned on all sides. This should take around 3 minutes.

2. If your slow cooker does not have this function, it is nice to do this in a large frying pan, on a high heat. Transfer the pork to the slow cooker bowl once browned.

3. Add all the remaining ingredients, cover with the lid and cook the pork on low for 6–8 hours until it is very tender and will fall apart with ease.

4. Serve the shredded meat atop mashed potatoes or white beans, as above. Serve a spoonful of the cooking liquid over the meat. Leafy greens, such as cavolo nero, also make a great accompaniment.

TIP

If you prefer more sauce, while making mashed potatoes the cooking liquid can be reduced by simmering vigorously in a pan until it is reduced to a third of the original volume. Spoon over the meat when serving.

serves
4

This casserole is very easy to make and full of flavour. It is such an easy dish to throw together and has the bonus of being a complete meal in one.

MEAT

Pork Sausage Casserole
with Celeriac and Kale

1 tablespoon olive oil
8 pork sausages
1 large red onion, sliced
1 large celeriac, peeled, trimmed and cut into 2 cm (¾ inch) cubes
4 garlic cloves, chopped
2 bay leaves
1 heaped tablespoon tomato purée
1 heaped tablespoon Dijon mustard

100 ml (3½ fl oz) red wine
200 ml (7 fl oz) chicken or vegetable stock (see page 113 for homemade)
250 g (8 oz) kale leaves, stalks removed and chopped
salt and pepper
10 g (¼ oz) flat leaf parsley, chopped, to garnish

1. If you have a sear or braise function on the slow cooker, switch it on and add the oil. Fry the sausages for a few minutes to brown them, turning them to get some colour around each sausage.

2. If your slow cooker does not have this function, it is nice to do this in a large frying pan, on a high heat. Once the sausages have been browned, transfer them to the slow cooker bowl.

3. Add the onion, celeriac, garlic, bay leaves, some salt and pepper, the tomato purée, mustard, wine and stock. Cover with the lid and cook on low for at least 3 hours until the sauce is rich and the sausages are fully cooked through.

4. Add the kale around 15 minutes before you want to eat. Stir it into the casserole and allow it to heat through.

5. Serve the hot sausage casserole garnished with the chopped parsley.

TIP

It is worth taking the time to brown the sausages. If you can do this while chopping the vegetables, it will make the prep even quicker.

serves
4

Pepperpot is a meat stew, often made using beef (and sometimes other meats), although there are several different styles of making this recipe. This one is inspired by Guyanese-style pepperpot, which features meltingly tender beef and a dark, sticky sauce.

Beef Pepperpot

1 tablespoon sunflower or rapeseed oil
500 g (1 lb) braising or chuck steak, cut into 3 cm (1¼ inch) cubes
1 onion, finely sliced
20 g (¾ oz) fresh root ginger, peeled and grated
1 red chilli or ½ Scotch bonnet chilli, sliced
1 cinnamon stick
½ teaspoon whole cloves
1 teaspoon black peppercorns

1 bay leaf
zest of 1 orange
100 g (3½ oz) dark brown soft sugar
100 ml (3½ fl oz) dark rum
1 teaspoon dark soy sauce
½ teaspoon salt
1 teaspoon Worcestershire sauce
100 ml (3½ fl oz) water
basmati rice, to serve

1. If you have a sear or braise function on the slow cooker, switch it on. Add the oil, beef, onion, ginger and chilli, then fry for a couple of minutes to start to get the dish cooking.

2. If your slow cooker does not have this function, it is worth taking the trouble to do this in a large frying pan on a high heat. Once the ingredients start to smell fragrant, transfer them to the slow cooker.

3. Add all the remaining ingredients, stir, cover with the lid, and cook on low for at least 6 hours until the meat is very tender, and the sauce is rich, thickened and dark in colour. Serve hot, with rice.

TIP

A seasoning called cassareep is often used to add colour and flavour to pepperpot, but I've substituted it for brown sugar, Worcestershire sauce and soy, which isn't the same, but these ingredients are much easier to get hold of.

serves
4

This fragrant stew is sure to please a crowd. It's fantastic served with mashed potatoes and a green vegetable of your choice.

Braised Lamb
with Red Wine, Orange and Green Olives

500 g (1 lb) shoulder of lamb, trimmed and cut into 3 cm (1¼ inch) chunks
3 tablespoons olive oil
1 large onion, quartered
1 leek, trimmed, cleaned and roughly chopped
1 carrot, peeled and cut into 3 cm (1¼ inch) slices on an angle
2 celery sticks, cut into 3 cm (1¼ inch) slices on an angle
8 garlic cloves, roughly chopped

1 sprig of rosemary
4 bay leaves
2 large oranges, zest peeled into strips using a vegetable peeler, and their juice
250 ml (8 fl oz) red wine
150 ml (¼ pint) chicken or vegetable stock (see page 113 for homemade)
75 g (3 oz) green olives, pitted
salt and pepper
20 g (¾ oz) flat leaf parsley, chopped, to garnish

1. If your slow cooker has a sear or braise function, use this now. Start by quickly frying the lamb chunks in the olive oil in the slow cooker. Alternatively, you can do this in a frying pan on a high heat. Add the onion, leek, carrot and celery and fry for a couple of minutes to start to soften the vegetables. Add the garlic, rosemary and bay leaves, and season well.

2. If you need to transfer the mixture from a pan to the slow cooker, do this now, and add the orange zest and juice, wine, stock and olives. Cover with the lid and cook on low for at least 4 hours until the meat is very tender. Taste and adjust the seasoning if you need to. Serve hot, sprinkled with the chopped parsley. Any leftovers will keep for up to 5 days in the refrigerator. This is also a great dish to make in advance and reheat by placing the slow cooker on the keep warm setting until you are ready to serve.

85

Extras, Sides and Snacks *Ideas*

Spiced Red Cabbage with Apple

Thinly slice 1 **red cabbage**. Put in the slow cooker with 2 **bay leaves**, 6 **star anise**, 1 **cinnamon stick**, 75 ml (3 fl oz) **apple cider vinegar**, 50–75 g (2–3 oz) **caster sugar**, depending on how sweet you like it, 2 thinly sliced **dessert apples**. Stir together. Put the lid on and cook on high for around 3 hours until the cabbage has softened but still retains some bite.

Poached Dried Fruits with Orange Blossom

Put 500 g (1 lb) **dried fruit** (apricots or apples are great) in the slow cooker and add 200 ml (7 fl oz) water, 1 tablespoon **clear honey**, 2 **bay leaves**, zest of ½ **unwaxed lemon**, 1 teaspoon each of **vanilla extract**, **orange blossom water** and **green cardamom pods**. Stir, cover and cook on low for at least 1 hour until the fruit is tender, plump and fragrant.

Dark Chocolate and Vanilla Fudge

Put the contents of 397 g (13 oz) **can condensed milk**, 2 teaspoons **vanilla extract** and 380 g (12 oz) **plain dark chocolate** (70%), broken into pieces, into a heatproof bowl. Sit inside the slow cooker and carefully pour boiling water into the slow cooker bowl, so that it comes halfway up the outside of the bowl of chocolate. Set the slow cooker to keep warm. Place the lid over, but prop it open, so it doesn't seal. Allow 30 minutes for the chocolate to melt into the condensed milk. Line a 20 cm (8 inch) square tin with nonstick baking paper. Stir the fudge mixture well and then pour into the prepared tin. Cover and refrigerate until firm and then cut into cubes. Store in the refrigerator in a sealed container for up to a week.

Note: If you have a searing slow cooker, you can make a traditional fudge recipe using the slow cooker bowl. Most recipes will need to get up to 112–115°C (234–239°F) – soft ball stage – to set, and this function will enable you to get the temperature high enough to fully set.

Roux

Melt 50 g (2 oz) **butter** in the slow cooker, set to high. Add 50 g (2 oz) **plain flour**. Stir in and keep stirring as the roux starts to bubble. Allow to cool. Transfer to a box and store in the refrigerator for at least 1–2 weeks. It will form a firm block once chilled. Grate it into sauces as needed to thicken.

Dumplings

Place 225 g (7½ oz) **self-raising flour,** 115 g (3¾ oz) **suet** and a large pinch of **salt** in a mixing bowl. Stir together. Add 5 teaspoons **creamed horseradish or mustard,** if desired, followed by 150 ml (¼ pint) cold water and start to bring the mixture together to form a moist ball. If it feels a little dry, sprinkle on another tablespoon of water. Form the dumpling mixture into round balls. If the mixture is sticky to work with, dampen your hands with cold water, which will make the mixture easier to handle. You should be able to make at least 8. To cook, take the lid off the slow cooker and sit the dumplings into a stew. Cover and cook on high for 30–45 minutes. They will feel firm when fully cooked.

Cauliflower Cheese

Melt 50 g (2 oz) **butter** in the slow cooker, set to high. Add 50 g (2 oz) **plain flour.** Stir in and keep stirring as the roux starts to bubble. Add 1 teaspoon **Dijon mustard,** some **salt and pepper** and 150 g (5 oz) grated **mature Cheddar cheese.** Stir in. Add 100 ml (3½ fl oz) **milk** and stir until smooth. Add another 400 ml (14 fl oz) **milk** and whisk until smooth. Cut 1 **large cauliflower** into florets, halving any large pieces. Put the raw cauliflower into the sauce. Cover with the lid and cook on high for 2–3 hours, stirring occasionally, if possible, until the cauliflower is tender and the sauce is gently bubbling, smooth and cheesy.

Slow-cooked 'Baked' Beans in a Tomato Sauce

Warm 2 tablespoons **olive oil** in the slow cooker set to high and add 3 peeled **garlic cloves,** 1 tablespoon **cumin seeds,** 1 teaspoon **salt,** some **pepper** and 250 g (8 oz) each of **canned butter or cannellini beans,** drained and rinsed, and chopped **tomatoes.** Add 100 ml (3½ fl oz) **vegetable or chicken stock** and cover with the lid. Cook on high for 2–3 hours until the beans are tender, but with a bit of squeak left. Serve hot or cold.

Glazed Carrots with Butter

Peel 500 g (1 lb) **carrots** and cut them on an angle. Put them into the slow cooker and add 100 ml (3½ fl oz) **vegetable or chicken stock,** 10 g (¼ oz) **butter** and season with **salt, pepper** and a **pinch of sugar.** Cook on low for 1–2 hours and stir occasionally, to ensure the carrots are coated in the buttery water. When the carrots are tender but retaining a little bite, either spoon them out of the slow cooker, leaving any liquid behind or continue to cook on low with the lid ajar until the excess liquid cooks off and they are slightly glossy. Either way, they will taste delicious.

Curries

serves
4

This is a wonderfully fruity and slightly sour curry, with punchy flavours from green chilli, tamarind and tomatoes. This recipe is very content simmering away very slowly in the slow cooker until required.

Chicken Madras

1 tablespoon sunflower or
   rapeseed oil
25 g (1 oz) butter
1 onion, thinly sliced
6 garlic cloves, chopped
3 tablespoons peeled and
   grated fresh root ginger
1 green chilli, deseeded and
   roughly chopped
10 fresh curry leaves
1 tablespoon black mustard
   seeds
2 tablespoons garam
masala, plus 1 teaspoon
   (optional) to serve
1 teaspoon salt
2 teaspoons tamarind purée
2 teaspoons brown
   soft sugar
400 g (13 oz) can chopped
   tomatoes
500 g (1 lb) boneless,
   skinless chicken thighs
basmati rice, or chapattis or
   naan, to serve

1. If you have a sear or braise function on the slow cooker, switch it on and add the oil and butter. Add the onion, garlic, ginger, chilli, curry leaves, mustard seeds, garam masala and salt and fry for a couple of minutes to cook the spices and soften the onion, garlic and ginger.

2. If your slow cooker does not have this function, it is nice to do this in a large frying pan, on a high heat. Add the tamarind purée, sugar, tomatoes and chicken and stir together.

3. Transfer the mixture to the slow cooker bowl, if you used a pan, then cover and cook on low for at least 4 hours until the chicken is very tender and the sauce has thickened.

4. Taste, adjust the seasoning with a little more salt or sugar if you feel it's needed. You can finish it with a sprinkling of another teaspoon of garam masala for a little more spice.

5. Serve with rice, or chapattis or naan. Leftovers keep well in the refrigerator for up to 5 days. Reheat thoroughly.

91

serves
4

While this is a more involved recipe to prepare, the result is wonderful and is worth every minute of work involved. When that's done though, the slow cooker will do the rest, and it produces a truly special curry.

Lamb Shoulder Curry

1 tablespoon rapeseed oil
2 onions, chopped
8 garlic cloves, chopped
3 tablespoons peeled and
   grated fresh root ginger
1 green chilli, deseeded and
   chopped
1 teaspoon whole green
   cardamom pods
2 bay leaves
½ teaspoon whole cloves
1 teaspoon black
   peppercorns
1 cinnamon stick
1 tablespoon ground cumin
1 tablespoon ground
   coriander
2 tablespoons garam
   masala

½ teaspoon ground
   turmeric
1 teaspoon fennel seeds
10 fresh curry leaves
1 teaspoon salt
1 teaspoon caster sugar
250 g (8 oz) tomatoes,
   chopped
500 g (1 lb) lamb shoulder,
   trimmed and cut into 3 cm
   (1¼ inch) chunks
200 ml (7 fl oz) canned
   full-fat coconut milk
20 g (¾ oz) fresh coriander,
   chopped
basmati rice, or naan or
   chapattis, to serve

1. If you have a sear or braise function on the slow cooker, switch it on and add the oil. Add the onions, garlic, ginger and chilli, followed by all the spices and the salt. Fry for a couple of minutes to get the onions, garlic and spices cooking.

2. If your slow cooker does not have this function, it is nice to do this in a large frying pan, on a high heat. Once the ingredients have been cooked for a few minutes, transfer them to the slow cooker bowl.

3. Add all the remaining ingredients, cover and cook on high for at least 4 hours until the the lamb is falling apart. Serve topped with the fresh coriander and rice or breads on the side.

A wonderful slow-cooked curry, which can be served either as a main dish or as a side. Either way, it's bound to be a hit.

Potato and Spinach Curry

1 tablespoon sunflower or rapeseed oil, or ghee
1 tablespoon black mustard seeds
1 tablespoon cumin seeds
1 onion, thinly sliced
6 garlic cloves, chopped
1 tablespoon peeled and grated fresh root ginger
1 green chilli, deseeded and chopped
1 teaspoon ground turmeric
1 teaspoon salt
200 g (7 oz) tomatoes, chopped

1 teaspoon caster sugar
175 ml (6 fl oz) water
500 g (1 lb) potatoes, peeled and cut into 5 cm (2 inch) chunks
100 g (3½ oz) fresh spinach leaves
10 g (¼ oz) fresh coriander, chopped
20 g (¾ oz) butter (optional)
pepper

1. If you have a sear or braise function on the slow cooker, switch it on and add the oil or ghee, mustard and cumin seeds, onion, garlic, ginger, chilli, turmeric and salt. Briefly fry for a minute or two to get the dish to start cooking.

2. If your slow cooker does not have this function, this can be done in a large frying pan, on a high heat. Once the ingredients have been briefly fried, transfer them to the slow cooker bowl.

3. Add some pepper, the tomatoes, sugar, measured water and the potatoes. Stir, cover with the lid and cook on low for 1–2 hours until the potatoes are tender.

4. Add the spinach and cook on low for 10–15 minutes until it's fully wilted. Stir in the coriander, just before serving, and the butter, if using. Season to taste and serve immediately.

serves
4

This is such a flavoursome dish, packed full of sweet and aromatic spices. Helpfully, it is really straightforward to prepare. Serve with rice or a flatbread to mop up the fragrant sauce.

Spiced Chicken *with Red Lentils*

500 g (1 lb) boneless, skinless chicken chunks, either breast or thigh
8 garlic cloves, roughly chopped
3 tablespoons peeled and grated fresh root ginger
1 heaped teaspoon ground cumin
1 heaped teaspoon ground coriander
1 heaped teaspoon fennel seeds
1 heaped teaspoon green cardamom pods
1 teaspoon fenugreek seeds

6 whole cloves
1 cinnamon stick
1 tablespoon sunflower or rapeseed oil
2 heaped tablespoons tomato purée
2 tablespoons tamarind purée
100 g (3½ oz) dried red lentils
600 ml (1 pint) chicken or vegetable stock (see page 113 for homemade)
20 g (¾ oz) fresh coriander, roughly chopped
salt and pepper
rice or flatbreads, to serve

1. If your slow cooker has the sear or braise function, use this now. Start by quickly frying the chicken, garlic, ginger and all the spices in the oil in the slow cooker. Alternatively, you can do this in a frying pan, on a high heat. Fry for a couple of minutes to start to cook the spices.

2. If you need to transfer the mixture back from a pan to the slow cooker, do this now. Next, add the tomato purée, tamarind purée, lentils and stock and season well.

3. Put the lid on the slow cooker and cook on low for at least 2 hours until the sauce is thickened, the chicken is tender and the lentils are soft. Taste, add a bit more salt if needed, and serve topped with the chopped coriander, and rice or flatbreads alongside.

Gentle in spice, but full of flavour, this is a really good stew to make at any time of the year. It's packed full of vegetables and popular with adults and children.

Spiced Chickpea, Sweet Potato and Spinach Stew

1 tablespoon sunflower or rapeseed oil
1 tablespoon black mustard seeds
1 tablespoon fenugreek seeds
1 tablespoon ground cumin
1 tablespoon ground coriander
1 heaped teaspoon salt
1 large sweet potato, peeled and cut into 3 cm (1¼ inch) chunks

2 x 400 g (13 oz) cans chickpeas, drained and rinsed
400 g (13 oz) can chopped tomatoes
1 heaped teaspoon caster sugar
100 ml (3½ fl oz) water
125 g (4 oz) fresh spinach leaves

1. Set the slow cooker to high. Add the oil and spices and fry for a minute or two as the slow cooker warms up. Add the salt and sweet potato and stir, coating the sweet potato in the spices.

2. Next, add the chickpeas and stir again, followed by the tomatoes, sugar and measured water. Stir again, cover with the lid and cook on high for at least 2 hours until the sweet potato is fully tender.

3. Just before you want to serve, add the spinach leaves and stir them through the stew so that they wilt. Taste and adjust the seasoning if needed. You may need a little more salt or sugar.

The flavours of turmeric, tamarind, curry leaves and coconut add so much depth and richness to this dish – it's extremely good.

Coconut Chicken
with Tamarind and Curry Leaves

1 tablespoon sunflower or rapeseed oil
1 onion, sliced
6 garlic cloves, chopped
1 tablespoon peeled and grated fresh root ginger
1 heaped tablespoon ground coriander
1 teaspoon ground turmeric
10 fresh curry leaves
1 cinnamon stick

500 g (1 lb) boneless, skinless chicken thighs, trimmed
1 tablespoon tamarind purée
1 teaspoon salt
1 teaspoon caster sugar
400 ml (14 fl oz) can full-fat coconut milk
basmati rice, or naan, paratha or roti, to serve

1. If you have a sear or braise function on the slow cooker, switch it on and add the oil, onion, garlic and ginger, together with the coriander, turmeric and curry leaves and fry for a minute or so to start cooking the spices.

2. If your slow cooker does not have this function, this can be done in a large frying pan, on a high heat. Once the ingredients have been cooked for a few minutes, transfer them to the slow cooker bowl.

3. Add all the remaining ingredients, stir well, the cover with the lid and cook on high for around 3–4 hours until the chicken is very tender. This dish will cook for longer on low very happily. Taste the sauce and adjust the seasoning if needed. Serve with rice or flatbreads.

If you have a stick blender or food processor, use it to make a paste to form the base of this curry. It's absolutely worth the effort.

Lamb, Tomato and Coriander Curry

1 tablespoon cumin seeds, toasted
1 tablespoon coriander seeds, toasted
1 large onion, quartered
6 garlic cloves, peeled
30 g (1 oz) fresh root ginger, peeled and roughly chopped
50 ml (2 fl oz) cold water
1 teaspoon sunflower or rapeseed oil

600 g (1¼ lb) lamb shoulder, trimmed and cut into 3 cm (1¼ inch) cubes
1 heaped teaspoon ground turmeric
1 teaspoon sea salt
1 teaspoon caster sugar
400 g (13 oz) can chopped tomatoes, liquid drained
20 g (¾ oz) fresh coriander, chopped
basmati rice, to serve

1. Start by placing the cumin and coriander seeds, the onion, garlic and ginger in a jug with a stick blender or a food processor and blend with the measured water until it forms a smooth-ish paste. Alternatively, the ingredients can be chopped by hand and then combined.

2. If you have a sear or braise function on the slow cooker, switch it on and add the oil and spice paste. Fry for a couple of minutes to get the dish to start cooking.

3. If your slow cooker does not have this function, this can be done in a large frying pan, on a high heat. Cook the paste for a few minutes, then transfer it to the slow cooker bowl.

4. Add the lamb, turmeric, salt and sugar, followed by the tomatoes. Stir well, cover with the lid and cook gently on low for around 4 hours, stirring regularly, until the lamb is really tender. It will cook for longer on low if needed. Serve with freshly cooked rice, and topped with the chopped coriander.

101

This is a wonderfully flavourful, simple dhal. It is delicious served on its own, perhaps with rice or some sort of flatbread as a simple meal, or to accompany a range of dishes. The tarka at the end is a lovely addition, but the dhal will still be good without it, if time is tight.

Tarka Dhal

CURRIES

FOR THE DHAL
5 garlic cloves, minced
5 cm (2 inch) piece of
    fresh root ginger, peeled
    and grated
250 g (8 oz) ripe tomatoes,
    chopped
300 g (10 oz) dried
    mung dhal
½ teaspoon ground
    turmeric
1 litre (1¾ pints) water
1½ teaspoons salt

FOR THE TARKA
4 tablespoons sunflower oil
2 teaspoons cumin seeds
1 teaspoon black mustard
    seeds
1 green chilli, finely sliced
12 fresh curry leaves

1. Place all the ingredients for the dhal into the slow cooker and cover with the lid. Set to high and cook for at least 2 hours until the lentils are very tender. The dhal can be served as it is, but it can be nice to lightly blend it, which is done most easily by using a stick blender.

2. Just before serving, make the tarka. Heat the oil in a small frying pan on a medium heat and, when it's hot, add the cumin and mustard seeds, green chilli and curry leaves. Heat for 30 seconds and then pour immediately on top of the dhal. Stir and serve.

serves
4

This curry is so popular and couldn't be easier to make. Simply adjust the flavourings at the end to suit your taste and serve with some freshly cooked rice.

Thai Red Chicken Curry

4 tablespoons Thai red curry paste
400 ml (14 fl oz) can full-fat coconut milk
500 g (1 lb) boneless, skinless chicken thighs, trimmed
2 red peppers, cored, deseeded and cut into 1 cm (½ inch)-thick strips
1 teaspoon brown soft or palm sugar
150 g (5 oz) green beans, halved

TO SERVE
fish sauce, to taste
freshly squeezed lime juice, to taste
10 g (¼ oz) fresh coriander, chopped
basmati or jasmine rice

1. Set the slow cooker to high and add all the curry ingredients, except the green beans. Stir well, cover with the lid and cook on low for at least 4 hours.

2. Thirty minutes before serving, add the green beans.

3. Taste the curry and add fish sauce for saltiness and lime juice for acidity, a little at a time until you are happy with the flavour. Top with the chopped coriander and serve spooned into bowls, with rice alongside.

This curry is so warming and savoury, with plenty of flavour from the fresh ginger and pepper. It's a real family favourite.

Chicken, Ginger and Tomato Curry

4 tablespoons sunflower or rapeseed oil

2 red onions, finely chopped

3 tablespoons peeled nd grated fresh root ginger

1 green chilli, deseeded and finely chopped

1 tablespoon cumin seeds

1 teaspoon ground turmeric

½ teaspoon black peppercorns

1 teaspoon sea salt

1 teaspoon caster sugar

1 heaped teaspoon garam masala

500 g (1 lb) boneless, skinless chicken thighs, cut into chunks

250 g (8 oz) tomatoes, chopped

150 ml (¼ pint) water

2 tablespoons chopped fresh coriander

basmati rice and/or naan, paratha or roti, to serve

1. If you have a sear or braise function on the slow cooker, switch it on and add the oil, onions, ginger, chilli, cumin seeds and turmeric and fry for a couple of minutes to get the dish to start cooking.

2. If your slow cooker does not have this function, this can be done in a large frying pan, on a high heat. Once the ingredients have been cooked for a few minutes, transfer them to the slow cooker bowl.

3. Add all the remaining ingredients, except the fresh coriander. Stir well, cover and cook on low for at least 4 hours until the chicken is tender and the tomatoes are very soft. Serve hot, topped with the chopped coriander and with plenty of rice and/or naan, paratha or roti alongside.

serves
4

This sensational dish is very much worth the time and effort. It is imperative to allow it to almost dry out, and for it to darken in colour towards the end of cooking. Make it in advance or for a crowd as it improves when reheated and served the following day.

Beef Rendang

2 tablespoons coriander seeds
1 tablespoon cumin seeds
1 large onion, roughly chopped
10 garlic cloves, peeled
20 g (¾ oz) fresh root ginger, peeled and roughly chopped
2 lemon grass sticks, outer layer removed, topped and tailed, and roughly sliced
1 tablespoon sunflower oil
1 long cinnamon stick
10 whole cloves
4 star anise
1 tablespoon ground turmeric

1 tablespoon green cardamom pods
4 tablespoons tamarind purée
2 tablespoons light brown soft sugar
1 tablespoon sea salt
600 g (1¼ lb) chuck steak, trimmed and cut into 3 cm (1¼ inch) cubes
400 ml (14 fl oz) can full-fat coconut milk
15 g (½ oz) fresh coriander, chopped (optional)
basmati or jasmine rice, to serve (optional)

1. Set your slow cooker to a sear or braise function (if you have one) and start by making the spice paste. If your slow cooker only has a high function, then set it to high and use a frying pan to fry the spice paste later on.

2. In a dry, nonstick frying pan, add the coriander and cumin seeds and fry on a high heat for a minute or two until fragrant. Remove from the heat when you can smell them, and they start to brown.

TIP

For best results, use a stick blender or food processor to make the curry paste.

3. Next, put the garlic, onion, ginger and lemon grass into a food processor, or use stick blender. Add the toasted coriander and cumin seeds and blend until smooth. You may need to add a couple of tablespoons of water to help the blender along.

4. Put the oil into the slow cooker (or into a frying pan on a high heat) and pour in the onion and spice paste. Add the cinnamon, cloves, star anise, turmeric and cardamom pods and fry for a minute or two to release the fragrance. Transfer the mixture back into the preheated slow cooker if you need to do this.

5. Now, add all the remaining ingredients, stir well, then cover with the lid and cook on low for at least 8 hours, stirring occasionally, if you can. After around 6–7 hours, the sauce will turn a rich brown colour, changing from the initial yellow coconut colour. The coconut milk will reduce significantly, leaving drier chunks of extremely tender beef. This is what you are aiming for.

6. Rest for 10 minutes before serving. Serve with some rice, if desired, and the chopped coriander on top, if you like.

serves
4
as a main course

This popular dhal is a real treat. The time to prepare this dish is required in intervals, with a few short bursts of activity throughout the cooking time, but each stage is very quick to complete.

Dhal Makhani

200 g (7 oz) dried urad dhal
   or black gram
50 g (2 oz) fresh root ginger,
   peeled and grated
1 green chilli, deseeded
   and chopped
50 g (2 oz) butter
150 g (5 oz) passata

(sieved tomatoes)
125 ml (4 fl oz) double
   cream, plus extra
   (optional) to serve
1 teaspoon salt
fresh coriander, to garnish
   (optional)

1. First, soak the dhal in cold water for around 8 hours, or overnight. Rinse thoroughly in cold water, drain and put into the slow cooker.

2. Add the ginger and green chilli, then just cover with water. Cover with the lid and cook on high for around 4 hours until the dhal is completely tender.

3. Drain, return the dhal to the slow cooker and add the butter, passata, cream and salt.

4. Cover and cook again on high for another 2–4 hours until the sauce tastes rich and has darkened a little in colour. Serve as a main course, or as part of a selection of dishes, with an extra drizzle of cream and fresh coriander, if you wish.

Basics *Ideas*

Homemade Yogurt

The key to success is maintaining warm conditions for the yogurt, which should be around 36–42°C (97–108°F). Some slow cookers have a yogurt-making function. A food-safe thermometer is very helpful for this recipe. Stir together 500 ml (17 fl oz) **milk** and 50 g (2 oz) **live natural yogurt** in the slow cooker. Cover with the lid. Set to yogurt mode and leave for 6–8 hours until the yogurt is thick. Transfer to a container and refrigerate to set. Alternatively, set the slow cooker to keep warm until the temperature of the milk gets to a maximum of 42°C (108°F). This will likely take around 30 minutes, but every slow cooker is different, so keep an eye on it the first time you make it. When the temperature has been achieved, turn off the slow cooker and put a couple of clean tea towels over it to trap in the warmth. Check after 6–8 hours, as above.

Breakfast Oats

This quantity makes 1 hearty adult portion – multiply as needed. Put 80 g (3¼ oz) **jumbo porridge oats** and 350 ml (12 fl oz) **milk** into the slow cooker. Cover, set to low and cook for 1 hour. Stir well to break up any clumps of oats and then spoon into a bowl.

You can swap some of the milk for water, if preferred. This is a great recipe to use your delay start function, so you can come down to warm, fresh porridge first thing.

Slow Cooker Dried Pulses

This recipe works for dried beans and peas, rather than lentils. Take 500 g (1 lb) **dried pulses** and place into a large bowl, covering with cold water. Soak for at least 8 hours, or overnight. Drain and rinse. Put the dried pulses into the slow cooker. Add twice the volume of cold water. Cover and cook on high for 2–6 hours until the pulses are completely tender. They will swell with water as they soak and cook. Taste and test the pulses to ensure they're cooked. They will keep stored in the refrigerator for up to 5 days.

Fluffy Rice

Serves 4. Put 250 g (8 oz) **white basmati rice** into a sieve and rinse well in cold water. Transfer the washed rice to the slow cooker. Add a generous pinch of **salt** and stir into the rice. Add 550 ml (17½ fl oz) cold water. Stir, cover with the lid and cook on low for 2 hours. Fluff up the rice using a fork before serving. You may also wish to stir a knob of butter into the rice.

Soda Bread

Take 2 large sheets of nonstick baking paper and line the slow cooker bowl with 1 sheet. Then set aside the second sheet on the work surface. In a big bowl, mix 275 g (9 oz) each of **plain white flour** and **plain wholemeal flour** with 1 teaspoon **salt** and 2 teaspoons **bicarbonate of soda**. Add 350 ml (12 fl oz) **thick natural yogurt** and 250 ml (8 fl oz) **milk** and stir in, then use your hands to bring the mixture together to form a ball, with all the ingredients incorporated. Dust the worktop with a small handful of flour and roll the dough into a ball. Transfer the ball to the centre of the second sheet of baking paper. Take a sharp knife and cut a deep cross into the dough, around three-quarters of the way through. Carefully lift the loaf on the paper and lower into the lined slow cooker, cover with the lid and cook on high for 2–2½ hours until firm. Flip for the last 30 minutes to achieve a slightly crispy top.

Chicken Stock

Put at least 1 **chicken carcass** into the slow cooker (if you have two or three, add them too) and add 1 halved **onion**, 1 halved **leek**, 2 halved **celery sticks**, 2 halved **carrots**, 1 teaspoon **black peppercorns** and 1 **bay leaf**. Just cover with water, cover with the lid and cook on low for around 3–5 hours, but longer is fine. Strain and use fresh or freeze. Store in the refrigerator in a sealed container for up to 5 days. Freeze for up to 3 months.

Vegetable Stock

Put 2 halved **onions**, 2 halved **leeks**, 3 halved **celery sticks**, 3 halved **carrots**, 1 teaspoon **black peppercorns** and 2 **bay leaves** into the slow cooker. Cover with 2.5 litres (4 pints) cold water, cover with the lid and cook on low for around 2 hours, but longer is fine. Strain and use fresh or freeze. Store in a sealed container in the refrigerator for up to 5 days. Freeze for up to 3 months.

Beef Stock

Put 1.5 kg (3 lb) **roasted beef bones**, 2 halved **onions**, 2 halved **leeks**, 3 halved **celery sticks**, 3 halved **carrots**, 1 teaspoon **black peppercorns** and 2 **bay leaves** into the slow cooker. Just cover with water and cook on low for around 3–5 hours, but longer is fine. Strain and use fresh or freeze. Store in a sealed container in the refrigerator for up to 5 days. Freeze for up to 3 months.

Note: Roasted beef bones make all the difference so if you are roasting beef, keep the oven on at 180°C (350°F), Gas Mark 4, once the meal is cooked, and roast the bones in a tray for an extra 45 minutes, then remove from the oven and use to make stock at a convenient time.

Sweet

serves
8

A real family favourite, this light and chocolaty pudding creates its own sauce as it cooks. It's extremely good served with some vanilla ice cream.

Chocolate Self-saucing Pudding

75 g (3 oz) butter, softened
100 g (3½ oz) caster sugar
150 g (5 oz) self-raising
   flour
50 g (2 oz) cocoa powder
1½ teaspoons baking
   powder
2 eggs, beaten
1 teaspoon vanilla extract

150 ml (¼ pint) milk
vanilla ice cream, to serve

FOR THE TOPPING
25 g (1 oz) cocoa powder
50 g (2 oz) light brown
   soft sugar
500 ml (17 fl oz) boiling
   water

1. Take 2 large sheets of nonstick baking paper and double-line the slow cooker bowl.

2. Place the butter, caster sugar, flour, cocoa, baking powder, eggs, vanilla and milk in a large mixing bowl and whisk together, ideally using an electric whisk. Whisk until thick, smooth and evenly mixed.

3. Set aside for a moment and mix the topping ingredients together in a jug.

4. Spoon the pudding mixture carefully into the lined slow cooker, ensuring it sits neatly inside the paper. Level off the top. Pour the liquid topping over the pudding batter.

5. Cover with the lid and cook on low for at least 1½ hours. The sponge will start to set and turn shiny, and the sauce will develop at the bottom of the bowl.

6. You may need to stick a spoon into the pudding to see how well cooked the sponge is. As soon as it is firm, with some liquid sauce underneath, it's ready to serve.

7. Spoon into bowls, serving it warm, with vanilla ice cream.

This slow-cooker rice pudding is deliciously soft and creamy. After 2 hours, it is fully cooked and quite liquid, which can be nice eaten hot. After 2½–3 hours, it has thickened more and the liquid has been absorbed, resulting in a firmer texture.

Vanilla, Lemon and Nutmeg Rice Pudding

100 g (3½ oz) pudding rice
750 ml (1¼ pints) milk
300 ml (½ pint) double cream
75 g (3 oz) caster sugar

1 teaspoon vanilla extract or bean paste
zest of 1 unwaxed lemon
¼ teaspoon ground nutmeg

1. Measure all the ingredients into the slow cooker bowl. It is quite nice to take the lemon zest off the lemon in big strips, using a potato peeler. These impart a lovely lemon flavour, but can be removed before serving, if preferred.

2. Cover with the lid, set the slow cooker to low and cook for 2–3 hours. If you can, give the pudding a stir or even a gentle whisk every 30 minutes or so, to ensure it cooks evenly, and the rice breaks up as it cooks. When the rice has swollen and is tender and the liquid has been absorbed, taste and check the rice is fully cooked and the flavouring is to your taste. Add more sugar, vanilla, lemon or nutmeg, if you like.

3. Serve hot or cold with fresh fruit, fruit compote, more cream or even some good-quality jam.

4. As the pudding cools, it will thicken further, especially so if it is left in the slow cooker bowl to cool.

If you're after a warming pudding that isn't too sweet, this could fit the bill. It has very little added sugar. You can, of course, add a little more if you prefer. It serves four with some left over for breakfast, which is nice with some thick yogurt and perhaps a little honey.

Pearl Barley Pudding
with Spiced Apples and Dates

250 g (8 oz) pearl barley
600 ml (1 pint) milk
500 ml (17 fl oz) water
30 g (1 oz) demerara sugar
2 apples, grated
75 g (3 oz) dates, pits
   removed and chopped
1 teaspoon ground
   cinnamon

1 teaspoon freshly grated
   nutmeg
zest of ½ unwaxed lemon

TO SERVE
cream or thick natural
   yogurt
a drizzle of clear honey

1. Simply place all the ingredients in the slow cooker, stir, put the lid on and set to low.

2. Cook for at least 1½ hours until the pearl barley is tender. Taste and adjust the flavourings, if you need to, perhaps with a little more sweetness or spice.

3. It is best to transfer the pudding mixture to a separate dish to cool, as it will continue cooking if it is left in the slow cooker.

4. If you prefer a softer result, you can add more milk and stir through.

5. Serve warm or cold with cream or thick yogurt and a drizzle of honey.

serves
8

This is a slightly unusual take on a cheesecake, but it's really popular. This is a recipe to make ahead, chill and serve.

Slow Cooker Cheesecake
with Coffee and Hazelnuts

500 g (1 lb) full-fat cream cheese
250 ml (8 fl oz) double cream
125 g (4 oz) caster sugar
1 teaspoon vanilla bean paste or extract
100 ml (3½ fl oz) brewed espresso, cooled
1 tablespoon hazelnut liqueur (optional)

2 eggs
25 g (1 oz) plain flour
50 g (2 oz) chopped roasted hazelnuts

TO SERVE
around 16 caramelized speculoos biscuits (I use Biscoff)
pouring cream (optional)

1. Double-line the slow cooker bowl with 2 large sheets of nonstick baking paper. The size and thickness of the cheesecake will vary depending on the shape of your bowl.

2. Put all the cheesecake ingredients into a mixing bowl and whisk together until smooth. Pour into the lined slow cooker, cover with the lid and cook on low for 1–2 hours until set. The time will vary, depending on the thickness. When there is no liquid mixture remaining in the centre, it is cooked.

3. Turn the slow cooker off and, when it is cool enough to do so safely, lift the cheesecake out and allow to cool. Then refrigerate, ideally overnight. The cheesecake can be eaten warm but is best chilled.

4. To serve, cut into slices or squares, and serve, topped with around 2 crushed biscuits per portion, sprinkled on top. You can serve with pouring cream too, if desired.

serves
8

This is such a winter treat, a traditional buttery steamed sponge pudding. The idea is to make a plain, steamed pudding, which is great served with all kinds of fruit, either fresh or poached, and cream or custard.

Vanilla Butter Steamed Pudding

250 g (8 oz) butter, softened, plus a little extra for greasing
250 g (8 oz) caster sugar
4 eggs, beaten

1 tablespoon vanilla extract
250 g (8 oz) self-raising flour
2 tablespoons milk

1. To make the pudding, set aside a 1.5-litre (2½-pint) pudding bowl that will fit inside the slow cooker. Lightly butter the inside of the bowl. Fill the kettle and boil it. If you have a rack to go inside the slow cooker, have that to hand, together with a sheet of nonstick baking paper and another of foil that will cover the top of the pudding bowl.

2. Beat the butter and sugar together in a bowl. Add the eggs and vanilla and whisk in, followed the flour and milk. Whisk until smooth. Pour the batter into the prepared bowl.

3. Take the sheet of baking paper and place the foil on top, shiny-side up. Fold a pleat in the middle of both sheets. Sit on top of the pudding bowl, foil-side up, pleat running across the widest part of the bowl, and scrunch down the sides of the bowl.

4. Sit the bowl inside the slow cooker. If you have a rack, put this in first and then place the pudding on top. Very carefully, fill the slow cooker with boiling water, so that it reaches roughly halfway up the side of the pudding dish. Place the lid on top and cook on low for around 4 hours until the pudding has slightly risen, is springy and no liquid batter remains. Serve warm, with fruit and cream.

TIP

For a twist, add a couple of tablespoons of jam, syrup or even berries to the bottom of the dish before adding the pudding mixture.

These cooked apples make an excellent pudding, perhaps served with yogurt, ice cream or even custard. They are very nice for breakfast, too, either with porridge or yogurt.

Slow-cooked Spiced Apple

6 large dessert apples,
    peeled, cored and sliced
25 g (1 oz) butter (optional)
50 g (2 oz) demerara sugar

1 cinnamon stick
½ teaspoon whole cloves
1 teaspoon vanilla extract

SWEET

1. Place all the ingredients in the slow cooker and set to low. Cover with the lid and cook for at least 2 hours until the fruit is soft and fragrant with the spices and butter.

2. Serve warm, with your choice of accompaniments.

TIP

You can substitute pears or quinces for the apples, but bear in mind that quinces takes longer to cook than apples or pears.

This all-in-one sticky toffee pudding combines the tender, sticky sponge and richness of the toffee sauce in one, making it very easy to make. It's guaranteed to delight anyone who loves this classic pudding.

Date, Treacle and Brown Sugar Sticky Toffee Pudding

200 g (7 oz) Medjool dates, pits removed and chopped
100 ml (3½ fl oz) boiling water
100 g (3½ oz) butter, softened
1 teaspoon vanilla extract
250 g (8 oz) light brown soft sugar

4 tablespoons treacle
2 eggs
175 g (6 oz) self-raising flour
1 teaspoon baking powder
250 g (8 oz) crème fraîche
crème fraîche, cream or thick natural yogurt, to serve

1. Take a large sheet of nonstick baking paper and sit it inside the slow cooker bowl in a central position.

2. Put the dates into a food processor and pour over the boiling water. Blend briefly to break up the dates. Next, add all the remaining ingredients and blend until the mixture looks even. It will become quite thick.

3. Carefully spoon into the lined slow cooker, sitting the mixture within the paper. Cover with the lid and set to cook on high for around 2 hours. Take a look now and then and check if the pudding has set and there is no wet batter in the centre. If the mixture is still wet, continue to cook for 15-minute intervals before checking it again.

4. Once cooked, turn off the heat and leave the pudding to firm up a little. Serve warm or cold with crème fraîche, cream or thick yogurt.

TIP

If you don't have a food processor, you can also use a stick blender in a mixing bowl. Or the mixture can be whisked together in a bowl until smooth, making sure the dates are finely chopped first.

This is an absolutely gorgeous pudding. I like to prepare the spiced plums in advance, and sometimes multiply the batch, as they are just so delicious with the rice pudding or just with some yogurt. They keep well in the refrigerator for up to 5 days.

Coconut and Lemon Sponge
Pudding *with Spiced Plums*

75 g (3 oz) butter, softened
200 g (7 oz) caster sugar
3 eggs
50 g (2 oz) desiccated coconut
125 g (4 oz) self-raising flour
zest and juice of 2 unwaxed lemons
100 ml (3½ fl oz) milk
cream, to serve (optional)

FOR THE SPICED PLUMS
500 g (1 lb) plums, cut in half and pits removed
50 g (2 oz) light brown soft sugar
1 cinnamon stick
2 star anise
1 tablespoon water

1. Start with the plums. Simply place all the ingredients into the slow cooker, cover and cook on low for around 2–3 hours until the plums are very tender and the juices have mixed with the sugar and spices. Serve warm or cold.

2. To make the pudding, set aside a 1.5-litre (2½-pint) shallow dish that will fit inside the slow cooker. A Pyrex dish is ideal. Fill the kettle and put it on to boil. If you have a rack to go inside the slow cooker, have that to hand.

3. Beat the butter and sugar together in a bowl. Add the eggs and whisk in, followed by all the remaining ingredients. Whisk until smooth. Pour the batter into the shallow dish.

4. Sit the dish inside the slow cooker. If you have a rack, put this in first and then place the pudding on top. Very carefully, pour in the boiling water, so that it reaches halfway up the side of the pudding dish. Place the lid on and cook on high for 1½–2 hours until the pudding has slightly risen, is springy and has no liquid batter remaining. Serve warm, with the spiced plums. Some cream makes a nice addition, too.

Made using the all-in-one method, this easy pudding is guaranteed to impress. The combination of chocolate, tahini and banana is wonderful. Serve warm – when it is soft and full of melted chocolate chunks – or cold.

Chocolate and Tahini Pudding
with Bananas and Cream

SWEET

3 ripe bananas, roughly mashed
50 g (2 oz) salted butter, softened
100 g (3½ oz) light brown soft sugar
1 egg, beaten
1 teaspoon vanilla extract
2 tablespoons tahini
5 tablespoons milk
75 g (3 oz) self-raising flour
2 tablespoons cocoa powder

½ teaspoon bicarbonate of soda
100 g (3½ oz) plain dark chocolate (70%), chopped, or chocolate chips

TO SERVE
sliced banana (optional)
softly whipped cream or pouring cream

1. Take 2 large sheets of nonstick baking paper and double-line the slow cooker bowl.

2. Add all the pudding ingredients, except the plain dark chocolate, to a large mixing bowl. Whisk together until you have a smooth batter. This is easier if you have an electric whisk. If you don't, add and whisk in the ingredients one at a time, following the order in which they are listed above.

3. Stir in the chopped chocolate or chocolate chips and pour the mixture into the prepared slow cooker. Level off using a spatula or the back of a spoon. Cover and cook on low for 2–3 hours until the pudding has firmed up (excluding the melted chocolate chunks, which will create little pools of chocolate). The top will look really glossy when cooked.

4. To serve, spoon from the slow cooker, or carefully lift out and cut into wedges. Serve warm or cold with slices of fresh banana, if you like, and cream.

130

serves
4
generously

A light, fruity and spicy pudding that's prepared in minutes. Ginger cream is a lovely accompaniment (see Tip), but it's also very good served with cream, vanilla ice cream or the Toffee Sauce on page 139.

Sticky Ginger and Pear Pudding

125 g (4 oz) butter, softened
125 g (4 oz) light brown soft sugar
1 teaspoon vanilla extract
2 eggs
50 g (2 oz) ground almonds
100 g (3½ oz) self-raising flour
350 g (11½ oz) ripe pears, (around 4), peeled, cored and chopped into 1 cm (½ inch) cubes
6 stem ginger balls, chopped, plus 3 tablespoons syrup from the jar
2 teaspoons ground ginger
4 tablespoons demerara sugar

1. Set aside a 1.5-litre (2½-pint) shallow dish that will fit inside the slow cooker. Pyrex is ideal. Boil the kettle. If you have a rack to go inside the slow cooker, have that to hand.

2. Beat the butter and soft brown sugar together in a bowl. Add the vanilla and eggs and whisk in, followed by the almonds and flour. Whisk until smooth. Stir in the pears and all the ginger. Pour into the shallow dish. Sprinkle with the demerara sugar.

3. Sit the dish inside the slow cooker. If you have a rack, put this in first and then place the pudding on top. Very carefully, fill the slow cooker with boiling water, so that it reaches halfway up the sides of the pudding dish. Place the lid on and cook on high for around 2 hours until the pudding has slightly risen, is springy and no liquid batter remains.

4. Serve warm.

TIP

For a ginger cream to serve, stir 2 chopped stem ginger balls, plus 3 tablespoons syrup from the jar into 125 ml (4 fl oz) whipped cream.

133

A classic steamed pudding packed full of fruit and spice. You'll be amazed how much better a homemade pudding tastes, compared to a shop-bought one.

Christmas Pudding

125 g (4 oz) butter, softened, plus a little extra for greasing
50 g (2 oz) light brown soft sugar
½ fresh nutmeg, grated or 1 teaspoon ground nutmeg
2 eggs, beaten
250 g (8 oz) sultanas
250 g (8 oz) raisins

100 g (3½ oz) mixed candied peel, chopped
1 small Bramley apple, cored and grated
1 tablespoon brandy, rum or whisky
25 g (1 oz) fresh breadcrumbs
60 g (2¼ oz) ground almonds
75 g (3 oz) plain flour

1. Start by buttering a 1.2-litre (2-pint) pudding bowl and set aside. Take a sheet of nonstick baking paper and another of foil that will cover the top of the pudding dish. Sit the foil, shiny-side up, on top of the paper and fold a thick pleat into the middle. Set aside.

2. Place the butter and sugar in a bowl and cream together until they are evenly combined. Add the nutmeg and eggs and beat until thoroughly mixed in.

3. Next, add the sultanas, raisins, candied peel, grated apple and alcohol and stir in, followed by the breadcrumbs, ground almonds and flour. Fold together to form an evenly mixed batter. Fill the kettle and put it on to boil.

4. Spoon the mixture into the prepared pudding bowl and level off the thick, richly fruited batter with a spoon or spatula. Cover with the pleated paper and foil, foil-side up, lining up the pleat across the widest part of the bowl. Scrunch the sides down around the edge of the bowl so that it sits snugly on top.

5. Lower the Christmas pudding into the slow cooker, then pour in the boiling water until it comes halfway up the sides of the bowl. Place the lid firmly on top and cook on low for 8 hours. Keep an eye on the pudding every couple of hours if you can to ensure the water is topped up and doesn't run dry.

6. The pudding is cooked when it is firm and no wet batter remains on top. Remove the pudding when it is safe to lift it out of the water, taking great care not to scald yourself with the hot water or steam. The pudding should easily slip out of the pudding bowl when cooked, but you may wish to run a small palette knife around the edge of the bowl to release it. Either eat the pudding warm or allow it to cool on a wire rack if it's being stored for another day. It will reheat by steaming again in the pudding bowl in the slow cooker (as above) on low for around 2 hours, or very quickly in a microwave.

These apples are absolutely delicious and are so useful to have in the refrigerator for a quick pudding or even to serve for breakfast, perhaps with yogurt and granola.

Poached Apples
with Vanilla, Brown Sugar and Cardamom

2 tablespoons light brown
   soft sugar
2 tablespoons water
1 teaspoon vanilla extract
1 teaspoon green
   cardamom pods

4 large dessert apples,
   peeled, cored and cut into
   5 mm (¼ inch) slices

1. Measure out all the ingredients you need and then prepare the apples, to prevent them from browning.

2. Place all the ingredients in the slow cooker and set to low. Stir well, cover with the lid and cook for at least 2 hours until the apples are tender and fragrant. You may wish to stir the apples a couple of times while they cook to ensure they are coated in the cooking liquid. Add a dash more water if they look like they are drying out. There should not be a lot of liquid in the slow cooker at the end, just a little sweetened juice.

3. Serve warm or cold. The apples will keep for up to 5 days, stored in a covered container in the refrigerator.

Preserves, Sauces and Drinks *Ideas*

Berry Compote

Put 500 g (1 lb) **mixed berries** (fresh or frozen) into the slow cooker. Add 1 tablespoon each of **lemon juice, granulated sugar** and water. Cover and cook on low for at least 1 hour until the berries are sweet and tender. If you wish to thicken the compote, mix 3 teaspoons each of **cornflour** and cold water in a small dish. Add to the compote, stir in and cook for another 5 minutes, stirring occasionally. Cool, then store in a sealed container in the refrigerator for up to 5 days.

Spiced Cranberry Sauce

Put 300 g (10 oz) **fresh cranberries**, the zest and juice of 1 **orange**, 110 g (3¾ oz) **light brown soft sugar**, 100 ml (3½ fl oz) **red wine**, 3 **bay leaves**, 1 **cinnamon stick** and 3 **whole cloves** into the slow cooker. Stir, cover and set to low. Cook for at least 1 hour until the cranberries start to pop. Turn off the heat and leave to cool in the slow cooker. It will thicken and become a little stickier. Remove the bay and cinnamon if you like before storing in a clean jar. Cool, then store in a sealed container in the refrigerator for up to 5 days.

Tomato Sauce

Put 50 g (2 oz) **butter** and 4 chopped **garlic cloves** into the slow cooker and set to high. Allow the garlic to cook and smell fragrant. Add 500 g (1 lb) chopped **tomatoes** (remove the skins first, if preferred, by submerging them in boiling water for a minute or two and then skinning). Add 1 teaspoon each of **salt** and **sugar**. Cover and cook for at least 2 hours until it smells rich. Cook with the lid ajar if you wish to make a thicker sauce. The sauce will be ready to use straight away, but it can also be blended and even sieved to make a smoother sauce. Store in the refrigerator in a sealed container for up to 5 days.

Apple Sauce

Place 3 **large dessert apples**, peeled, cored and sliced, 1 tablespoon water and 1–2 tablespoons **sugar** into the slow cooker, cover and cook on low for at least 2 hours, stirring occasionally, to check the fruit softens and does not dry out. 2 sliced **plums** make a nice addition too. When the fruit is tender, mash it a little for a chunky sauce, or purée until smooth. For an extra layer of flavour, add a small **sprig of rosemary** and/ or a small knob of **butter**, if desired. Serve warm or cold. Store in a sealed container in the refrigerator for up to 5 days.

Toffee Sauce

Pour 300 ml (½ pint) **double cream**, 1 tablespoon **treacle** and 60 g (2¼ oz) **light or dark brown soft sugar** into the slow cooker. Set to low. Cover and cook gently, stirring occasionally, for around 1 hour until it is sticky and smooth. Serve the sauce warm, but keep any leftover sauce in a sealed contrainer in the refrigerator for up to a week and warm again to use it.

Mulled Wine

Put 750 ml (1¼ pints) good-quality **red wine**, the zest and juice of 1 **large orange**, the zest of 1 **unwaxed lemon**, 1 teaspoon **vanilla extract**, 75 g (3 oz) **caster sugar**, 6 **star anise**, 6 **whole cloves**, a good grating of **fresh nutmeg** (around 1 teaspoon) and 1 **cinnamon stick** into the slow cooker. Stir well, cover and warm through on low for at least 1 hour until the sugar has dissolved and it is hot. Taste and adjust the sweetness, if needed. Strain through a sieve if preferred and serve hot. This mulled wine will hold wonderfully well in the slow cooker, making it an ideal choice for entertaining.

Hot Chocolate

These measurements make 1 mug. Multiply the quantities as needed. Put 250 ml (8 fl oz) **milk**, 1 tablespoon each of **double cream** and **light brown soft sugar** with 25 g (1 oz) chopped **plain dark chocolate** (70%) into the slow cooker. Cover and warm on low for at least 1 hour. Whisk well until the colour looks homogenous. Ensure it's hot enough to drink comfortably and serve. It will hold using the keep warm function.

Winter Apple Punch

These measurements make 1 cup. Multiply the quantities as needed. Put 200 ml (7 fl oz) **cloudy apple juice**, 1 **cinnamon stick** and 2 **whole cloves** into a saucepan. Add 1 teaspoon **rum or whisky** if you would like an alcoholic version. Add 1 teaspoon **clear honey** if you would like extra sweetness. Cover and warm on low for 1 hour until it's hot and tastes pleasantly warming and sweetly spicy. It will hold using the keep warm function.

Index

141

UK/US Glossary

UK	US
Baking paper	Parchment paper
Bicarbonate of soda	Baking soda
Black beans	Turtle beans
Butter beans	Lima beans
Baking paper	Parchment paper
Bicarbonate of soda	Baking soda
Chestnut mushrooms	Cremini mushrooms
Chickpeas	Garbanzo beans
Coriander (fresh)	Cilantro
Cornflour	Cornstarch
Demerara sugar	Light brown sugar
Desiccated coconut	Dried shredded coconut
Double cream	Heavy cream
Dried chilli flakes	Crushed red pepper flakes
Electric whisk	Electric beaters
Flour, plain/self-raising	Flour, all-purpose/self-rising
Foil	Aluminium foil
Frying pan	Skillet
Grated	Shredded
Ground almonds	Almond meal
Jam	Preserves
Jug	Pitcher
Minced beef	Ground beef
Natural yogurt	Plain yogurt
Pak choi	Boy choy
Pepper	Bell pepper
Plain dark chocolate	Semi-sweet chocolate
Porridge	Oatmeal
Pudding bowl	Baking mould
Rapeseed oil	Canola oil
Spring onion	Scallion
Stem ginger	Preserved ginger
Stock	Broth
Sultanas	Golden raisins
Swede	Rutabaga
Sugar, caster	Sugar, superfine
Tea towel	Cloth kitchen towel
Tomato purée	Tomato paste
Treacle	Black molasses

Acknowledgements

Editorial Director: Natalie Bradley
Project Editor: Vicky Orchard
Art Director: Yasia Williams
Designer: maru studio G.K.
Photographer: Charlie Bard
Food Stylist: Henrietta Clancy
Props Stylist: Tamsin Weston
Production Managers: Nic Jones and Lucy Carter